4/19/80

495

Collecting Roots & Herbs for Fun & Profit

Martha Sherwood

Produced by Greatlakes Living Press
of Waukegan, Illinois,
for Contemporary Books, Inc.

Contemporary Books, Inc.
Chicago

Library of Congress Cataloging in Publication Data

Sherwood, Martha.
   Collecting roots and herbs for fun and profit.

   Bibliography: p.
   Includes index.
   1. Botany, Economic. 2. Herbs. 3. Wild plants,
Edible. 4. Botany, Economic—United States. 5. Wild
plants, Edible—United States. I. Title.
SB107.S43   1978   581.6'3'0973   77-91190
ISBN 0-8092-7675-5
ISBN 0-8092-7674-7

Illustrations by Nancy J. Schneider,
Bensenville, Illinois

Published by Contemporary Books, Inc.
180 North Michigan Avenue, Chicago, Illinois 60601
Manufactured in the United States of America
Library of Congress Catalog Card Number: 77-91190
International Standard Book Number: 0-8092-7675-5 (cloth)
                                    0-8092-7674-7 (paper)
Published simultaneously in Canada by
Beaverbooks
953 Dillingham Road
Pickering, Ontario L1W 1Z7
Canada

For Sean and Heather,
  Heather and Sean,
Equal in patience,
  That I might write this book.

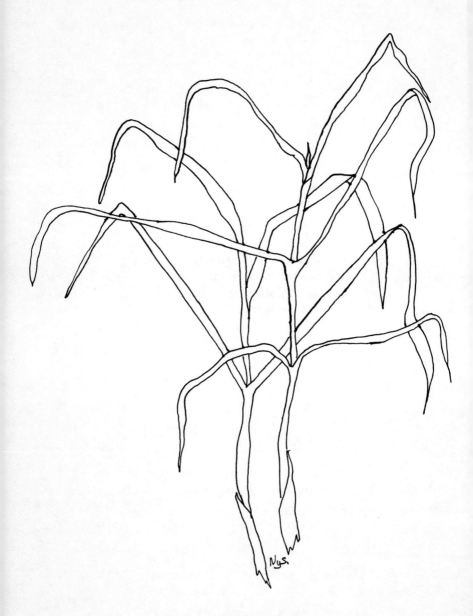

Lemongrass

Contents

Silverweed

1

Herbs and Roots

Herbs are weeds with a purpose. Nutritional. Medicinal. Cosmetic. Functional and lots of fun in a wide variety of ways, they are well known by those people who do not cringe at the sight of a suburban lawn full of dandelions, but who envision wine instead. Herbs grow in meadows and bogs, along road sides, in rich forest soil or mediocre dirt. They creep along the ground, float in water, huddle under larger plants, or tower over garden walls.

Roots are the underground gems whose greenery may or may not be useful. Second only to God, as they were considered by a 15th-century naturalist-missionary, they contain the essence of a life older than our own species. There are some root systems still thriving today that were alive at the time Aristotle was cultivating his 300-herb garden (384-322 B.C.).

Herbs are as diverse as their uses and as easy to

read as a road map once you know the key. It is said that you can tell how to use a plant by what it looks like—the botanical "what-you-see-is-what-you-get" theory. Called "the doctrine of signatures," this mystical element of herb lore stems from the belief that all is part of the One and One is all—that nature has meaning and, if we but read these signs, we will know, among other things, how to cure ourselves of aches, pains, and other ailments. Later in this book, we will go beyond this level of lore to what may be gaining new ground in medicine—*herbalism,* the study and use of plants for medicinal purposes.

The parts of herbs used in making teas, infusions, poultices, potpourris, and other derivations of these green "giants" are many. The ways plants are used is a science based on credible fantasy. During the renaissance, when astrology was enjoying the heyday it approaches now, it was believed that each sign of the zodiac affected a different part of the body. When it was discovered—by trial, error, and instinct—that different plants affected corresponding body parts, herbs and astrology were cast into a family circle with man and woman as the doting child.

But herbs were known and honored long before the stars got into the act. The oldest *herbal*—a book pertaining to the use of herbs—was a work by the Chinese emperor Shen-Nung, who supposedly lived to be 1040 years old. This is in some doubt, however, as the Orientals, who venerate age, have a tendency to increase respect by adding a few years. Egypt had 2,000 herb doctors 2,000 years before the beginning of the Christian era. Roman soldiers carried herbs on the march and herbs were used and cultivated across the continent. The renaissance saw the practice of herb cultivation expand beyond gardens of royalty and religious orders and into gardens and the kitchens of commoners.

At the same time, the Indians of North America were finding uses for herbs. And when European settlers came, the Indians shared their herbal wisdom. In turn, the Indians received what knowledge the newcomers had, and together the meld became the basis for American folk medicine. Birch bark tea became a remedy for weak limbs, and sassafras berries, a cold tonic. Today, more than 100 species of plants have cousins in chemistry that are taken by millions of Americans each year as pills and syrups prescribed by qualified physicians.

Folk medicine remains alive in Appalachia, and is spreading. Modern Americans are filling their homes with green, growing things, harvesting city plots, and giving up the urban jungle for country lanes. These new people following age-old customs are learning to live with and to love the natural way of life through herbs.

This book is written for those of you who would like to join the throng. You probably know the words to "Scarborough Fair" and how to use parsley, sage, rosemary and thyme. Now you can learn more. Let me introduce you to comfrey, cattails, ginseng, goldenseal, seaweeds, and tansy.

Herbs are found everywhere. You've probably been pulling them up and sneering at some of them as "weeds" for years. You may have suspected every three-leaved plant of harboring a dose of itch. It is time you knew what you were doing; it is time to pay attention to something other than such garden staples as corn, tomatoes, and green peppers. Add spice to your life; add herbs.

In the pages that follow, you will find an eclectic super stew of herbs and what they do. Chapter 2, "The Goods . . . ", will introduce the herbs that are good for you, that not only make you well when you are ill, but better when you feel fine. You will learn how to identify and prepare herbs such as sunflower, kelp, and others, some of which are almost complete foods containing essential vitamins, minerals, and other body-building ingredients. There are recipes for teas, coffee substitutes, and bath water.

Chapter 3, " . . . For What Ails You" provides information on a number of popular herbs and what they have been called on to cure over the years. Mix and match, faith and herbs, and chances are the prescriptions are accurate.

Herbs are for the present, to be sought out in the underbrush and to be planted in neat patches alone or among the vegetables at the doorstep. Chapter 4 gives instructions on "rooting around" to find herbs in the wilds and takes you for a romp in the woods. Chapter 5, "Herbs Inside/Out" begins with a fantasy tale that ends up telling how to plant an herb garden indoors or out.

Most of us are more familiar with dried herbs than fresh. Chapter 6, "Picking, Preparing, and Preserving," explains how to prepare and store herbs—dried, frozen, and even canned.

One of the categories of herbs is the aromatics—those that perfume our baths and bodies, freshen our linens, and keep the bugs out of the house. In "Mixed Bag," Chapter 7, you will discover how these sweet-smelling things are also being used to cure our emotional ills.

There will come a time when you have grown enough herbs for yourself and given away as many as family and friends will take. Chapter 8 is the next step, unloading the goodies locally and nationally. From door to door—to market to market—there are outlets for your greens and the products you make. Meet Bonnie Fisher of West Virginia who, with her husband, runs a cottage industry built around herbs that they sell at arts and craft fairs across the state.

Finally, like everything else, herb enthusiasts are organized. There are national associations and local clubs of herb enthusiasts. Chapter 9 provides a run-down on some "who's" in the herb world, including herbalist teachers, who are preparing others to offer us an alternative to chemical medical care. Perhaps, herbs may offer you a new career as well.

This eclectic approach to herbs describes each herb in appearance, location, preparation, and use. Some herbs will be mentioned without details, as to do so would turn this into an encyclopedia and leave no room for other information. At the end of this book you will find a list of other handbooks on herb identification and use. Where available, we have provided the retail market value for individual herbs. These prices should be considered as guidelines only, for the herb market varies, sometimes daily.*

Along the path of this book you will meet those in the mainstream—diggers, cultivators and suppliers, gardeners, and gatherers. Interjected throughout is a little philosophy, a touch of humor, and a few far-out facts. Help yourself. Take a pinch or a pocketful. Herbs are as fun as feathers in a bed, as old as time. They also are a constantly reviving, refreshing way of life.

An herb is to:	hunt	smell
	learn	cure
	see	eat
	pick	love
	taste	

*The prices quoted for herbs are based on market value during the summer of 1977. Market demand and availability determine value and may well have changed by publication date. You may get current prices from herb and seed companies or by writing to the Superintendent of Documents, U.S. Government Printing Office, Washington, D.C. 20013, and asking for current farmer's bulletins listing market values of crops.

2

The Goods . . .

"Eat it. It's good for you."
"Build strong bodies 12 ways . . . "
In the elementary nutrition pumped into us through parents, advertising, and school health programs, did anyone ever even mention herbs? Not to me. Parents in every American home worry their children constantly about eating properly, but where is the appeal to "eat your sunflower seeds" or "don't leave the kelp on your plate; think of all the starving children in the world." Perhaps, if we had grown up eating more of these things, our own bodies would now be lacking less in the way of wholesome nutrients.

Happily, it isn't too late to begin.

Alfalfa

Also called *lucerne, buffalo herb,* and *snail clover, alfalfa* is found across the Midwest. A perennial that,

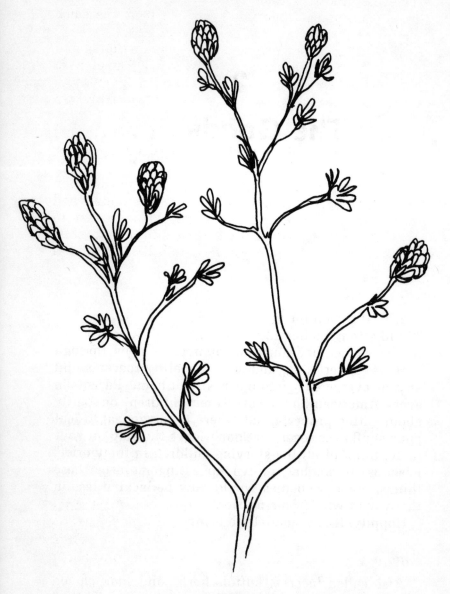

Alfalfa

when blooming, carries spiked violet flowers shaped somewhat like clover blossoms, alfalfa is a prolific grower springing three times or more from the same root in a year.

Harvesting takes place when the plant is young and tender, during the spring or early summer. The plant is hung up to dry, then taken down to be stripped of its seeds and leaves, the latter of which may be made into tea with equal parts of spearmint leaves. Or ground into a powder, it may be mixed with vinegar and honey and taken as a tonic, sprinkled on cereal, or mixed with soup and juices.

As a tonic, alfalfa is said to be a boon to the brain and spinal cord. It contains from 14 to 16 minerals and all known vitamins. Sprouted, alfalfa adds zest to vegetable salads, is an interesting addition to cole-slaw, and is a novel touch to oatmeal. It is truly a nutritive and tasty herb.

MARKET VALUE $2 per pound retail for tea.
$4.64 per pound retail for leaves.

Sunflower

Another wonder food is sunflower (Helianthus annus), that tall, nodding border flower found in country and city garden alike. A native American, sunflowers are easy to identify. They stand above all others, sometimes 12 feet tall. Daily their faces follow the course of the sun, drinking in its goodness and transforming it into food.

An economically perfect plant, there is no part of the sunflower that cannot be used in some way. The flowers contain a yellow dye. The oil is good for salads, cooking, making margarine, and even for burning in lamps. The stems contain fiber that can be made into paper; a medicinal infusion of the stems may be made and used as a treatment for malaria. The pith of the stalk, lighter than cork, can be used in life belts. And any leftovers can be fed to livestock or, as ash, used as a nutritious mulch for potatoes and other root crops.

Sunflowers are planted in the spring, two to three feet apart for seed production, wider for shading other crops. The mammoth Russian variety matures in 80 days; smaller heads, which are easier to harvest, take less time.

As the plants mature, the heads grow heavy and often need to be staked up for support. In late summer or early fall, when two-thirds of the seeds are filled and the birds have begun to help themselves, cut off the heads at the end of two to three feet of stalk. Hang the stalks to dry in an airy place. After a good, long drying time—just when you have almost forgotten about them—remove the seeds by gently brushing your hand over the sunflower's face.

Sunflower seeds contain calcium for strong teeth and gums, and roasted, they are a coffee substitute. They contain practically the whole spectrum of important nutritive elements—every vitamin except C and even that when sprouted. They are 25 percent protein, have more iron than egg yolks, and may be used for an occasional meat substitute. (When combined with grains, beans, and other seeds, all eight essential amino acids become available and the protein increases by up to 42 percent!)

The sunflower, which once crowned the temple priestesses of the Incas, is rapidly becoming an international commodity. Only now are U.S. farmers following the Russians and others in trading this perfect product. As a business, sunflower growing is a healthy one. An acre of sunflowers produces between 2,500 and 4,000 heads or 160 pounds of potash per acre. The tall heads that are 15 inches across produce about 50 gallons of oil to the acre and 150 pounds of oil cake, a

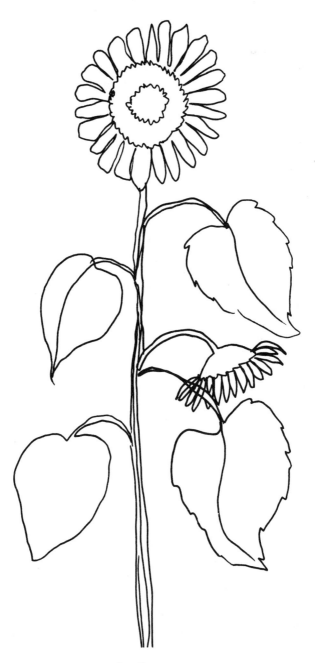

Sunflower

livestock feed. Then there are the packets of sunflower seeds strategically placed near the check-out counter at health food stores and supermarkets. It is truly a strong, beautiful flower, a life-giving food, and a highly marketable product.

Market Value

The Northern Sun Products Company of Gonvick, Minnesota, buys sunflower seeds in lots of one to two tons from individual farmers (FOB delivery). From this crop, which in a good year could render a farmer $60 to $80 an acre (competitive with wheat prices) in seed alone, they make a cooking oil that sells at about $1.75 retail for 1½ pints. Another sunflower product is a 30 percent protein stock feed. A flour for human consumption is being developed.

Kelp and Agar

The edge of the sea provides plants that may become the staples of the future—if sea farming takes hold in a big way. To most of us, they are just seaweeds, but kelp and agar, to name just two, are nutritious gifts from the sea.

Kelp *(Laminariales, Fucales)* is a plant body with a true root, stem, and leaves. Growing near the surface of the Pacific and the Atlantic, it is a rubbery, rope-like plant in shades of khaki brown and green. It attaches itself to rocks or mussels by means of extended tendril tips. One plant has many branches and can spread for yards.

Collection of kelp takes place at low tide, around the new, full moon, between the low and high tide marks on Pacific coastal beaches or in the mouths of New England bays. Kelp is a fast grower—up to 2 feet per day.

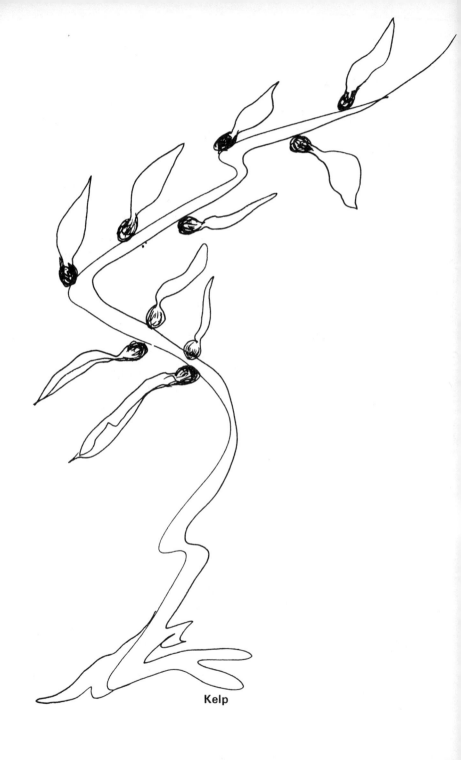

Kelp

Kelp contains calcium and sulfur, manganese, iron, copper, vitamins C, A, B complex, D, K, and E. It is a chief source of iodine, and it is high in chlorophyll. Resistant to pollution, it remains a perfect food despite its environment.

Kelp is said to aid dieters in correcting obesity, to remedy irregularities in the thyroid gland, cleanse the arteries, clear up severe headaches, and relieve anemia. Because of its silicone content, it may even provide a natural face lift! It is even reported to strengthen the jawbone, providing a natural resistance to dentures. It is said to be extremely valuable to pregnant women.

Kelp is collected with sickles or by light tugging and is sun-dried on racks in the open air. Powdered, it may be packed into 10-grain gelatin capsules or drunk as a tea. One tablet per day or one ounce of powdered kelp in a pint of boiling water (steeped 15 minutes) may be taken daily. As a vegetable, cook with carrots for a delicious side dish.

Kelp's full potential is yet unexplored. It has been written that kelp offers protection from radioactivity by letting the body resist the absorption of certain poisons given off by nuclear experimentation and by eliminating those poisons once they are absorbed. Japanese researchers have found that edible seaweeds of other varieties reduce cholesterol levels in the blood of laboratory rats.

Another sea treasure, a cousin to kelp, is agar (*Gelidium, Gracilaria, Eucheuma*). An alga found along the California coast, agar is collected in summer and autumn and spread out in the sun to bleach and dry. It is then boiled and strained through cheesecloth. The liquid is cooled in long, flat pans until it forms a gelatin-like substance, which is then cut into strips and again dried in the air and sun (but in a colder area to prevent the growth of bacteria and mold).

Agar, eaten in powdered form on stewed fruits, provides nonnutritive bulk, as a treatment for constipation. As a marketable item, agar has a variety of uses. Flavored, it may be sold as a vegetable gelatin providing an excellent dessert that is not only nutritious but also is easy to digest. Agar is sold to research laboratories for use as a culture medium. In slightly different form it also is sold to makers of ice cream, candies, and jellies for use as a thickening agent.

The following recipe may be made by sea souls and landlubbers alike from wakame kelp. This palatable dish requires reeducation of mind and palate, but considering its nutritive wealth, it is worth the try.

Wakame Soup

Immerse and soak 2 to 3 ounces of dried kelp in 5 to 7 cups of water.* Set aside to expand sevenfold.

Sauté 2 thinly sliced onions in sesame oil until transparent.

Remove kelp from water and add water to sauteed onions. Bring to a boil.

Slice kelp into small pieces and add to boiling water; reduce heat.

Simmer 20 minutes or until kelp is tender.

Remove from heat and add miso paste or cubed bean curd, if you like. (The miso tends to make it a bit more salty, I find).

Serves 4 to 5 adults.

MARKET VALUE $8.48 per pound retail for kelp.
$8.32 per pound retail for hizuki.
$10.08 per pound retail for wakame.

---

*You may substitute chicken or vegetable broth for the water. Or try kelp in a chowder with potatoes, onions, and milk.

Jerusalem Artichokes

An old root that is regaining popularity is the *Jerusalem artichoke (Helianthus tuberosus)*. Neither from the Holy Land nor a member of the family of that stiff floral vegetable, the traditional artichoke, the Jerusalem artichoke is a cousin to the sunflower and was called the "sun root" by the Indians.

Its flowers resemble those of its cousin, but they do not have the large, brown, seed-full centers. Instead, its food value is below ground, at the foot of its stalk, which grows five to eight feet wild, in waste places, or 10 to 12 feet when cultivated. The Jerusalem artichoke is found in open, wet places and grows well in most areas of North America. Its leaves are oval and opposite, and its large yellow flowers have greenish centers in the autumn.

Jerusalem artichokes are planted as you would potatoes, either in the spring or the fall. They do well in limed or composted soil but need no extra care. They may be planted, as you would sunflowers, along the edges of your garden; they also make a good shade row for plants such as lettuce, spinach, and swiss chard.

Having no natural enemies, the Jerusalem artichoke spreads wildly. It can be controlled by digging up the tubers in the spring and separating them into new rows. (This also improves the quality of the tuber.) Collect what you need in autumn and leave the rest in the ground. The plant winters perfectly in frozen ground and is ready to use immediately after a thaw.

Although often likened to potatoes and used similarly, Jerusalem artichokes contain no starch. Eaten raw, they have a nutty flavor. They may be boiled, baked, pureed (with peas and the like), added to soups and stews and pickle relish. They are good with mushrooms or spices and butter. Bake them thinly sliced with wild onion and cheese. Cooking time is not more than 10 minutes, and the cooking water makes a good soup base.

Jerusalem artichoke

Jerusalem Salad

Grate Jerusalem artichokes and add to a mixture of shredded cabbage, grated carrots, raisins, and chopped apples. Flavor with sorrel, lovage, or parsley.

Artichoke Chips

Thinly slice Jerusalem artichokes. Toast on a cookie sheet with butter and lemon juice.

Jerusalem artichokes are a cash crop, too. They out yield the potato, producing up to 15 tons per acre compared to the potato's three.

To start from scratch you may order Jerusalem artichoke seeds from Geo. Park Seed Company, Greenwood, South Carolina 29647 ($3.50 per pound) or William Dam Seeds, West Flamboro, Ontario L0R 2K0, Canada (10 tubers for $1.95; 25 for $4.50).

MARKET VALUE   Price is comparable to potato prices.

Sprouts

The wonder-foods category expands with the addition of sprouts. All the nutritive powers of the plant are concentrated in the seed. The life of the plant is released in the sprout.

Alfalfa, soybeans, garbanzo beans (also called chickpeas), sunflower, sesame, fenugreek—all types of beans and seeds may be sprouted. Never use those sold for gardening and farming. They have been chemically treated and can make you ill at the very least. Buy your seeds at the local health food store or order them directly from the supplier. (See Chapter 4 for a listing of companies that sell seeds. Be sure to indicate that you want them for sprouting purposes.)

To sprout, place a quarter cup of seeds in a quart jar

and fill halfway with cool water. Soak eight hours. Pour off the water and preserve it for use in steaming vegetables, as a soup base, or for cooking rice. Now cover the mouth of the jar with nylon or cheesecloth, secure with a rubber band, and lay the jar on its side. Let it rest in a warm place. Rinse the sprouts two or three times daily (save this water for your house-plants), and at the end of three days your sprouts will be ready for soups, salads, omelettes, and whatever other ingenious ways you might find to serve them. (I've seen them sprinkled on the top of open-faced peanut butter sandwiches!) For fun and bodily enrich-ment, try the following recipe:

Sprout Snack

Grind 2 cups of soy or garbanzo sprouts and 1½ cups of roasted peanuts together in a meat grinder or blender.

Combine with ¾ cup powdered milk (½ cup nonin-stant) and ¾ cup water. Set aside.

In another bowl mix 1 cup raw and ½ cup toasted sesame seeds and 1½ cups raw sunflower seeds, 1½ cups rye flour and ½ teaspoon sea salt.

Cut in ¾ cup peanut butter.

Mix sprout and seed mixtures together.

Separate in two and spread each half on an oiled cookie sheet.

Cover each section with a piece of wax paper and roll to ¼-inch thickness.

Remove wax paper.

Bake at 275° (F) for one hour or until brown.

Remove from oven. Cool and cut or break into squares (makes 60).

Serve as a family or party snack, or package and label with a personal stamp and sell to health food stores or at club and community fund raising events.

Teas

The most popular herb "goodie" is tea. Taken as a work-break beverage instead of coffee or as an offering of hospitality to unexpected house guests, tea's healthful properties are often overlooked.

Most herb teas have tonic qualities, so it is important to know what each is meant to do. (For example, do not take a purgative such as rhubarb root for a headache.) Do not drink herb tea excessively. Unless you are treating yourself for a malady or building yourself up with a tonic over a short period of time, use in strict moderation.

According to reports, too, teas taken with meals may interfere with the absorption of iron and may lead to vitamin B^1 deficiency. Vegetarians especially are susceptible if their protein intake is scant and their tea consumption totals four to six cups a day. The key, then, is to take the right tea at the right time and in the right amount.

Tea is an infusion of an herb in hot water. The water need not be boiling; excess heat may destroy important nutritive properties. Follow these steps for a proper herb tea:

Use fresh or dried herbs in bulk rather than in tea bags.
Use earthen, porcelain, enamel, or iron for the pot— never aluminum.
Use spring or well water if at all possible. The chemicals added to city tap water may undo all the good you are getting from the herbs.

Pour one cup hot water over a heaping teaspoon of herbs in a cup. Steep five minutes, no more. Drink hot and immediately. Allowing tea to stand does nothing for the flavor, and although iced tea is appealing, especially in hot weather, it is less therapeutic and nutritive than hot tea. When brewing a pot, trust your taste or follow the old rule of ½ teaspoon for each cup and one for the pot.

Tonics

Tonics originated in the days when spring cleaning was a standard practice and rugs were beaten with a wire whip that looked like the back of an ice cream parlor chair. Tonics still can do what they have always done—give us a boost when the winter chill has turned the blood to sludge.

Here are a few tonic herbs; information is included on where they are found and what "goods" they will give you. But don't just believe me. "Take tea, and see."

Burdock

Leading the spring warm-up list is burdock (*Arctium lappa*). A naturalized citizen, this three- to four-foot high, dull green plant has rough, heart-shaped leaves and a deep furrowed stalk. It is found along road sides and in waste places. Its flowers are clustered purple tubulars. The fruit is oblong, flat, and angular. In autumn it earns its name by producing sticky burrs.

But its root, which shoots down 12 inches and is one inch in diameter, is usually why the plant is cultivated. Roots are dug with a slender spade in the fall of the first year's growth (this plant has no flower stalk). The root is ground and dried. The tonic is made of 1 ounce ground root to 1½ pints of water (boiled down to a pint). It is one of the best for purifying the blood when taken in the fall and is a general and nutritive tonic in the spring.

If you'd prefer to drink beer and toast your own health, here's how:

Burdock

Burdock Beer

Collect 1 quart fresh burdock root, wild sarsaparilla, and spikenard.

Scrub clean and slice lengthwise, cutting into ½-inch pieces.

Boil 6 quarts of water containing fresh roots until the liquid is reduced to two quarts.

Strain;

Cool slightly;

Add 1 pint of molasses, ½ pound of sugar or honey, and yeast enough to make it work (ferment).

Ferment three to four days.

Bottle and store in a cool place.

MARKET VALUE   Burdock yields up to 2,000 pounds dry root per acre.
$1.50 to $3 per pound retail.

Barberry

Also called *Rocky Mountain grape* or *Oregon grape root*, barberry *(Berberis aquiqalium)* is found along the west coast of the U.S., in the moist soil of the Pacific

Barberry

mountain ranges, and in New England. It is a hardy wood shrub, an independent that needs little care—just enough sun and rain to give its yellow-gray stems a boost to its six- to ten-foot height. It has small-toothed, yellow flowers and either purple or yellow berries, depending on the variety.

A good general improvement tonic taken in small doses, barberry is said to renew vitality and to bring the nutritive processes back into balance, or, in other words, smooth out the system of digestion and elimination.

The bark of the plant is picked in the late fall and powdered, and an infusion of one-fourth teaspoon is taken three to four times a day.

MARKET VALUE $5 per pound retail.

Damiana

To aid and abet one's energy—to reduce that run-down feeling manifested in shaking and quaking at the knees—there is Damiana *(Turnera aphrodisiaca)*. Found in California, Texas, and Mexico, the plant is a small shrub noticed by the Conquistadors with mint-like, yellowish, fragrant flowers and smooth, pale green (topsides) leaves. Damiana smells sweet, tastes bitter, and makes a healthful tea that is said to encourage romantic dreams.

MARKET VALUE $5 per pound retail.

Chamomile

If yellow had a taste it would be *chamomile*. A timeless tea and tonic, chamomile conjures up visions of sweet old ladies and overstuffed armchairs. This is the herb of humility, a low-to-the-ground, creeping

Chamomile

plant that thrives when stepped on, a surefire ground cover in heavily trafficked areas around the house.

Chamomile's flowers are daisy-like, with yellow disks and creamy petals—18 rays to a sunny center. Its leaves give it a fragile, feathery look.

A plant physician, chamomile's first patients are other plants. Where chamomile grows, it tends its neighbor's needs by contributing to the health of the soil and keeping away pests.

You may start chamomile seeds in May, in a sunny spot, in soil of no special quality. Seedlings may be thinned the following March. Collect the blooms in late summer and dry them in an airy place away from direct sunlight.

To make a tea—which is also said to be a relaxant, a sedative, and to prevent nightmares—bring one cup of water to a boil, drop in two teaspoons of dried flowers, shut off the heat, and cover. Steep ten minutes. Strain, drink, and relax. Its dusty, apple-like fragrance and flavor may be improved with a little lemon.

Chamomile as a tonic is said to be good for the gastrointestinal tract, stomach disorders, and neuralgic pain. Soaked flowers may also be used as a poultice for relieving pain in external areas. As a lotion it may be applied for toothache, earache, and other nerve pains.

MARKET VALUE $ 1.50 to $3.25 per pound retail.

Elder

To clean out the metabolic wastes of winter, elder (*Sambucus canadensis*) makes a good spring tonic. Elder is found beside wooded brooks in moist, rich, and shaded soil. It bears dark purple berries preceded by creamy fragrant blossoms in flat clusters that appear in June and July. Growing to a maximum of eight

Elderberry

to twelve feet, its leaves are large and dark green. Elder may be propagated by cuttings of bare shoots in the fall.

The berries are picked when ripe, allowed to dry in the attic while still on the stem, and made into wine or jelly in combination with apples, grapes, or raspberries. The blossoms are picked in late spring and may be added to scrambled eggs and pancakes.

As a tea, elder flowers come into their own. One teaspoon of elder flowers to one cup of water, covered, and boiled in a pan for ten minutes, is drunk on an empty stomach one-half hour before breakfast every morning for two to three weeks as an April-May pick-me-up.

Elder also acts as a general diuretic, soothes the nerves, and was used by gypsies for head colds and as an eyewash. Its leaves, when bruised, keep flies away. Elder was known as "the tree of music" to the Indians, who made flutes of its branches.

MARKET VALUE $7.24 to $8 per pound retail for flowers.

Sassafras

An American herb, *sassafras* (*Sassafras officinale*) or *cinnamon wood* or *ague tree* provides a good general bodily housecleaning, when used in moderation. Sassafras contains *safrol,* a toxic that constitutes six to nine percent of its total composition.

Sassafras grows along the Eastern seaboard. In the South, the trees climb to 100 feet! Its slender branches host oval leaves and tiny greenish-yellow flowers.

It is the root—or, more precisely, the bark of the root—that is collected, dried, and prepared as tea. Used very infrequently alone or in combination with other, less pleasant-tasting blood purifiers, sassafras

Sassafras

provides a super spring tonic—one teaspoon to one cup chopped root.

One of the first commercial exports of this country, sassafras remains today a native and natural tonic. People who want to quit smoking sometimes find that a strip of sassafras bark is a good pacifier.

MARKET VALUE $5.16 per pound retail.

Herb Tea Combinations

Alfalfa and mint—contains vitamins A, D, E, K
    and the minerals calcium, iron and manganese
Lemon balm—flavors fruit drinks and iced and
    other teas
Chamomile—a natural sedative
Basil, rosemary, sage—relieves a headache
Rose petals—contains Vitamin C, calcium,
    manganese, and iron
Catnip and fennel—dispels gas
Catnip and sage—relieves a cold

Ginseng

The king of herbs—as myth, as tonic, as marketable root—is *Ginseng (Aralia quinquefolia)*. Once prolific in New England and the Midwest, ginseng has all but been wiped out by overcultivation in those areas. Now, it grows wild in the South, where diggers go into the rich woodlands, into the dappled shade on the slopes of mountain ridges to hunt the precious and evasive plant.

The ginseng plant grows slowly. Its first appearance, 18 months after planting, resembles that of a wild strawberry. The first year, two leaves cling to a stiff stalk; each leaf looks like a five-fingered hand. The second year it has four leaves and is ten inches high.

Now, reaching toward maturity, a second stem appears at the four-to-five-year mark with the same number of leaves. If allowed to grow longer, after ten years a third stem, and then a fourth, will grow out of the heart of the plant. Ginseng flowers are pale lilac with filaments like raw silk. The berries, appearing in the fall, are round and red.

It is the part below ground that matters—the ginseng root. Centuries ago people connected shapes of plants to curing whatever they looked like. Ginseng is shaped like a man's body, so it was associated with man's sexuality, thus becoming an aphrodisiac for males. The Chinese prescribe it for all disorders of the lungs and stomach (as well as to allay fear and to build character). As a nutritive, it normalizes the entire system, encouraging a healthy appetite and calming a quaking stomach caused by mental or nervous exhaustion. Ginseng is also said to prolong life. There's virtually nothing that believers in ginseng think this herb does *not* benefit or cure, including double vision, dizziness, headache, backache, hiccoughs, and pimples.

Chinese ginseng is touted as the best, but an investigation of the American market finds much of our native root being shipped abroad. The U.S. exported $5 million in ginseng in 1970; by 1976 the figure was $18 million. Most is shipped to the Far East.

North American ginseng was first discovered by Father Joseph Lafitau, a missionary who returned from China and went to work among the Mohawks of Canada. Knowing of its popularity in his former homeland, he used the Indians to gather the valuable root and started exporting it back to China in 1717. By the late 16th century, the hunt was on, with pioneers turning "sang hunters" overnight. The gold rush had nothing over ginseng for making and breaking individuals and fortunes. By 1800, ginseng turned up in patent medi-

North American ginseng

cines; soon diggers were scouring the Catskills, the Poconos, the Alleghenies, and the Appalachians for the sang.

American ingenuity being what it is, and laziness being a parallel trait, homebodies got wise and started to plant ginseng out the back door. Ginseng gardens sprang up between 1889 and 1905 and were centered in Amberg, Wisconsin, and Chardon, Ohio. Later the centers were shifted to New York and Michigan. Today the center of the cultivated ginseng industry is Marathon, Wisconsin. Some 65 farmers there grow 95 percent of the cultivated U.S. crop. (Wild ginseng trade accounts for 26 percent of U.S. production.)

Ginseng farming was a matter of bedding the root under lattice-shaded or vine-strung wire mesh gardens. But what took two years under a tree took seven years under wood slats and chicken wire, and the tamed root did not have the spunk of the wild kind. The same is true today, and many ginseng diggers try to grow the root without making it appear as though it is a cultivated crop. This is done by planting in the root's natural habitat—rich, shaded soil among poplars and walnut trees, under grape vines, or in the middle of a blackberry briar patch—and fertilizing with chicken manure from four to five feet away. But it is risky, as other diggers might poach the crop, and buyers are shrewd enough to nose out the cultivated from the wild. The wild root is smaller and more firm; the cultivated is oversized and pithy.

Industrialization, the advance of the population, and the run on the root in its heyday and to the present has made ginseng a dwindling commodity in the North. The supply is estimated to have dropped 20 percent in the last 10 years. It is still being hunted and dug in Missouri, West Virginia, Kentucky, and especially in North Carolina, Tennessee, and Georgia. In fact, in 1977 ginseng was put on the endangered species list by the U.S. government. Exports of wild ginseng have been banned, except by persons licensed by certain states to dig the root.

Those who live close to the land and care about the extinction of a botanical live by a special code of ethics when it comes to tracking sang.

1. Dig in the spring *only* if you intend to replant in beds close to home.
2. Dig in the fall only after the berries are ripe and the plant has come full circle (last of August at the earliest). Otherwise the root will be wrinkled and pithy, lack character, weight, and salability.
3. Sell the big roots; transplant the little ones.
4. Plant the berries where you take the root and scatter the others in the immediate area.
5. Dig up three prong roots only.

Sang hunters are a breed apart, secretive and a bit mysterious like the root they hunt. With their haver-pokes swinging by their sides and a stick or steel sang hoe at the ready, they wander the woods in search of sang.

Sang Cure-all

Grind up the roots of several plants;
Drop a handful into a short jug of white lightening;
Light it with a match;
Blow it out;
Take a l-o-n-g swig.

" . . . if it don't do you some good, you better get to a doctor and pretty durn fast!"
—Buck Carver, Appalachia*

Foxfire 3 (Garden City, N.Y.: Anchor Press/Doubleday, 1975).

The Chinese never hunt ginseng with an iron implement. They feel the root is best dug with the hands to preserve all the tendril roots that make ginseng visually valuable.

Ethics of hunting notwithstanding, ginseng is a profitable business. In 1907 it brought $12,000 per acre (of third-year growth). In 1977 the price per pound for dried wild root was $80. That's why it's a costly cup of tea.

The average wild root weighs six ounces. The average digger can collect two pounds a day. It takes five pounds of fresh root to produce one cured pound. So it's possible to collect almost $27 per day—not bad for a walk in the woods.

Ginseng is to be found, and you could make a tidy living at it—depending on how hard you work. But rather than gathering, you might consider farming.

The state of Pennsylvania has experimented with cultivation of ginseng for profit. The results in five years, starting from seed or set-ups, was a profit of $1,500, less the land cost per acre. The crop needs great care and special cultivation methods. The soil needs to be loose and rich with a heavy leaf mulch and 80 percent shade to duplicate its natural growing conditions as closely as possible. There is obviously something to ginseng farming for Johnny Bates, a Pittsfield, Illinois, cultivator: "To go out after it in the woods you might as well go to town, get a drink and a headache and get it over with," he says.

Bates farms ginseng between the Illinois and Mississippi rivers in western Illinois. He leaves the headaches of digging and gathering wild ginseng to others. But, listening to his story, he has a few headaches of his own.

I started in on ginseng about 12 years ago. I used to deal in livestock, and I was lookin' around for something different to do. A ginseng dealer told me where they raised some roots so I looked it over. I started with the wild roots, but that's kind of a slow way to get going, so I bought seeds from a place in northern Wisconsin. They originally came from Canada.

Bates farms about three and a half acres in ginseng, the rest in corn and hogs. It is a slow return on what he estimates would be today a $12,000 investment for seed, artificial shade, materials, and labor.

The first year you get nothing. It takes four to five years for a crop to come in, and in the meantime there is a lot of hard work and worry. He says from experience:

> The guy who doesn't understand it could get into a lot of trouble. You gotta understand what sprays to use, which insects to fight. You gotta fight it pretty hard, gotta know what to do at the right time.

Bates finds that between mice and moles and blight like the kind that hit with a spell of hot, muggy weather in the summer of '77, you've got to work hard not to lose your shirt. "It's not a get-rich-overnight deal," Bates admits, but his tone suggests that if there weren't something a bit mystical about raising the root, it would not be worth the trouble.

After four to five years of yanking weeds and fighting off the menaces, he says, "If you have good luck, you oughta get a ton of dried roots out of an acre."

On the market, that's $30 to $40 per pound for cultivated root. Then there is the seed, the bonus to be sold before the root is pulled. Bates, who sells to Magee, has tried selling abroad, where the money is, but "I haven't had much luck overseas; they got that wrapped up pretty tight. Magee is a good buyer."

According to Bates, however, not all buyers are as honest as Magee. Somebody else owes him $7,500, and "I can't run him down," he says.

The international market seems to be a good one if you can get into it. "The Chinese can't raise good ginseng; the climate don't suit it," Bates says. "Manchurian ginseng—I've never seen any of it—is supposed to be the highest priced. American comes next. Korean is at the bottom. Oh, there's some Russian ginseng and some other junk. American people think Korean is wonderful, but really American ginseng is better. Well," and he pauses like a puzzled farmer who does not understand the big fuss about his crop, "I don't really know if any of it's worth anything." Apparently, you can not prove it by Johnny Bates. He just grows it.

So, that's ginseng farming from a singular point of view. In contrast to running it down wild, it "keeps the bills paid up."

MARKET VALUE   Wild—$80 to $82 per pound retail for dried roots.
Cultivated—$30 to $40 per pound retail for dried roots.

Tea is the most popular form in which to use ginseng. Mixing the tea with night cream, ginseng becomes a cosmetic moisturizer and skin astringent. By adding just enough to basic cold cream to thin it slightly and massaging it into the face well, the complexion takes on a youthful glow and you have saved yourself the fuss of a face-lifting.

Other herbs recommended as tonics for the weight of age, the world, and winter are coriander, columbo, fire weed, gentian root, hyssop, lavender, magnolia, marjoram, prickly ash, turkey corn, wild cherry bark, yellow dock, fring gree, poke root, angelica, apple tree bark, heal-all, red clover blossoms, boneset, sweet flag, scullcap, wood betony, vervain, white pond lily, ginger, capsicum, bitter root, balcomy, poplar bark, golden-seal, white willow, black horehound, broom, centaury, comfrey, cudweed, ground ivy, dandelion, valerian, meadow sweet, mistletoe, red raspberry leaves, yar-row, sage, and giant Solomon's seal.

A Dip in Thyme and Other Baths

Herbs need not be eaten or drunk to be good for you. They may be soaked in through the pores of the skin as you rest in a tub of fragrant water.

Balneology is the art of bathing for health. Like any other art form, it takes time to learn properly. So, leave the showers to the jocks and learn the simple luxury of time in a tub. Bathing can be a spiritual experience when done in leisure and with the right herbs to set the stage for a water meditation.*

Selecting the right herb in which to bathe is as important as choosing the right tea to drink. I tried an invigorating soak in the essence of pine needles one evening between work and a weekday party and was up until 4:00 A.M—and the party ended early! For that time of day, I would suggest a bath in water doctored with powdered skim milk or steeped rasberry leaves.

Anise

Anise (Pimpinella anisum) is recommended for leis-urely dips in the tub. Cultivated in Rhode Island and other East Coast states, it grows to a height of 13 inches and has an erect cylindrical, striped stem. Its

---

*You can get in touch with the essence of water while sitting high and dry. Breathing in through the nose and out through the mouth while concentrating on the color green, you will be able to feel as though you were sitting under a soft waterfall. Take in the cleansing essence of water as you breath in, and let it wash through you. Then, as you exhale, feel the coolness, as though water were dripping from your fingertips and taking the body's impurities with it.

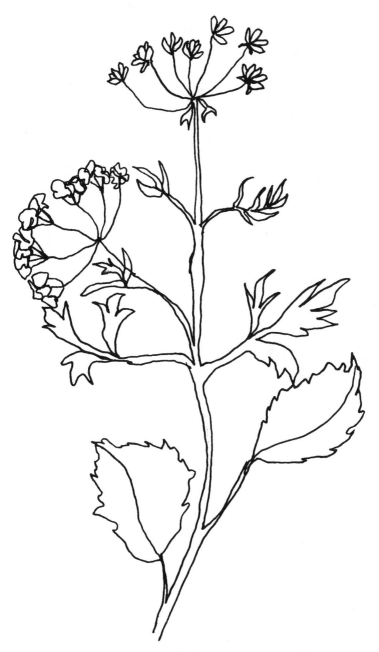

Anise

flowers are small and white and its seeds are shaped like a mouse with a pointed head. The plant has upper and lower leaves; the upper leaves grow opposite each other on short, feather-like stems; the lower leaves are egg-shaped and are found on longer stems.

Anise may be started in dry, light soil indoors and replanted outdoors in May or planted outdoors in late April.

MARKET VALUE $.86 to $2.25 per pound retail.

Rosemary

Rosemary

Rosemary (*Rosmarinus officinalis*) comes out of the garden, out of the kitchen, out of the ranks of nobility and into the beauty of the bath. Started in good rich soil indoors in January, it may be transplanted outside when the weather warms. It is a slow grower, taking perhaps three years for a bush to develop from seed. For this reason and because the germination percentages are not high for this plant, start with cuttings if possible. A six-inch tip of new growth from an established plant buried four inches into sand or vermiculite should do well. Water well and protect from winter weather by planting along a south wall of a house, covering with burlap or baskets during the cold months.

One-third teaspoon each of anise, rosemary and mint will make a pleasant mouthwash.

MARKET VALUE $4.75 a pound retail.

Marjoram

Marjoram (*Origanum marjorana*) is a tonic, too, although it is probably more popular in the U.S. as a culinary herb. Because it comes from the warm Mediterranean where it is a perennial, it must be started anew annually (indoors in flats) in this country. Transplant after the frost is gone. Marjoram's furry oval leaves branch off from a 12-inch square stem. By midsummer, white or pink flowers appear. It should be picked as the blooms thrive, dried, and stored.

MARKET VALUE $6.72 per pound retail.

Other scents recommended for the bath are lemon thyme, cardamon, spearmint, and lavender. Take a handful (about ½ cup dried) herbs and tie in a bit of cheesecloth or an old nylon stocking. Steep in a quart of boiling water for ten minutes and add the fragrant water to the tub water. Or, steep the loose herbs in water and strain the scented water into the tub. (Using flower petals and leaves—steep a cupful of mixed floral herbs in two cups of boiling water for 15 minutes. Strain and pour the liquid into your drawn bath.)

Immerse yourself, feeling the movement of the water, and smell the garden scents. Let thoughts flow by you as a stream ripples around stones. You will return to the world feeling good inside and out.

Massage: The Need to Knead

If the tub is too small to share an herb bath with a friend, why not exchange herbal massages? You may prepare a number of oils in advance. The herbs used in oils, like those in baths, should be selected for the result intended. Wash two to three sprigs of lavender, basil, lemon thyme, lemon verbena, or rose geranium (experiment with mixtures). Place the clean sprigs in a bottle of low-odor rubbing alcohol. Cap and set the bottle aside for 10 days; remove the sprigs and use the oil for massages or in quantities of one to two tablespoons in a hot tub.

St. John's Wort

The most highly regarded massage oil is made from St. John's wort (*Hypericum perforatum*). Found along the roadside, this herb grows to between one and three feet tall and has sun-bright flowers and black-spotted leaves. These spots contain the oil used in the massage. Strip the plant of its leaves, accumulating a quarter of a cup. Drop leaves into a bottle and pour a quart of olive oil over them. Allow to stand until the oil is reddish in color. A rub with St. John's wort will tighten the skin and produce an exhilarating effect. As a side effect, this herb is said to exorcise evil spirits.

MARKET VALUE $6.75 a pound retail.

Herbs to Launch a Thousand Ships

The shelves of health food stores and even pharmacies abound with soaps scented with avocado, strawberry, sweet woodruff, and other beautifying herbs. Using an aromatic herb (lavender, rose, and so on),

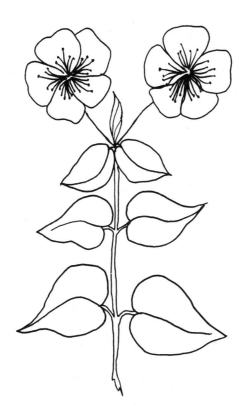

St. John's wort

you may prepare a cold cream as described in the section on ginseng. By adding 40,000 and 50,000 units of vitamins A and D from capsules purchased at a pharmacy to four ounces of a base cream, you may head off premature wrinkles.

For the look of Isis, the Egyptian goddess of fertility, try the following lotion. Carefully warm a cup of buttermilk into which you have put a mixed handful of elder flowers, marigold petals, geranium leaves and (believe it or not) a chopped clove of garlic. Simmer 40 minutes. Remove from heat, allow to cool, and set aside for five hours. Reheat and add one ounce of honey. Cool, use, and store.

Egyptians also used a skin conditioner made of pansies, chickweed, cleavers, meadowsweet, and scarlet pimpernel. Steep three or more of these herbs in water, making an infusion of them. Rinse the face with the infusion and allow to air dry. A good treatment for blemishes, it also will improve skin tone and texture. For specific treatment of blemishes, make a tincture (using alcohol) from any of the above herbs and apply directly with a cotton swab.

For a fast facial, pour boiling water over a fistful of herbs in a large bowl. Place a towel over your head and hold your head over the bowl. Inhale deeply. After 10 to 15 minutes, splash your face with cold, clear water.

For normal skin—try basil leaves, chamomile flowers, cloves, or peppermint.

For oily skin—use lemon grass, lavender flowers, rosebuds, rosemary, or sage leaves.

For dry skin—use clover tops or elder flowers.

Of course, a good complexion starts with clean hair. After shampooing, rinse your hair with an infusion of horsetail and sage. It will bring out the luster and natural color of the hair.

You can make your own shampoo:
Simmer 4 ounces soapwort bark chips in 2 cups of distilled water until water has been reduced to half. Cool. Strain. Add a few drops of your favorite herbal oil. Bottle. Use. You can market this as a natural product for those who care about their hair.

Sage

Once a noted medicinal herb, sage *(Sage officinalis)* remained popular as a culinary herb when worldwide herbal practices waned. In the 1600s the herbalist Gerard recommended sage as a tonic for head and brain, and it remains in use as a "cure" for nervous headaches.

Sage grows to a height of one foot or more with a square stem and round to oblong leaves. Sage's purple flowers appear in August. A perennial, sage winters well, but it should be brought in after three to four years to prevent it from turning into a woody shrub. It can be started from seed (a foot apart) after the last of winter outside or inside four weeks earlier. It grows well planted near rosemary. Harvest the upper leaves and stems in late summer or early autumn, through September at the latest. (If you can't remember all these little details about sage, take a bit in tea and, like rosemary, it will improve your memory.)

MARKET VALUE $8.10 per pound retail.

A Nightcap

The best cosmetic is a good night's sleep. The body does its repair work and the soul takes a vacation during sleep. To lure the sometimes evasive cloak, try one of the following:

Stuff a pillow with hops
Drink an infusion of lettuce (1 cup) before bedtime;
Pour a pint of boiling water over some grated fresh
    nutmeg and add a pinch of valerian.
Or, prepare a nightcap tea from pennyroyal, chamo-
    mile, boneset, damiana, dwarf elder and pepper-
    mint, hops, horehound, linden, or valerian. Rest
    easy and awake refreshed. It beats sleeping pills.

Pennyroyal

Pennyroyal *(Hedema puleogioides)* is found along the Atlantic coast and west to Texas and the Dakotas. A foot-tall annual, its stem is squarish with tiny flowers that bloom in the leaf axils. Pennyroyal should be started from seed in rich soil. It grows well in sun or shade and it needs plenty of water. Pennyroyal is best used fresh but it may be dried for later use.

MARKET VALUE $2 per pound retail.

Horehound

Horehound *(Marribium vulgare)* thrives in wild places and is often found in poor, dry ground. Although widely cultivated, it grows less well in northern climates. Horehound grows as a bush and branches annually with one to two feet of new growth. White flowers spring from where the creased leaves with furry hairs meet the stem. The leaves are harvested and used fresh or dried for nightcap tea.

MARKET VALUE $6.05 per pound retail.

Pennyroyal

Horehound

To horehound tea add:
a pinch of cayenne,
a dash of vinegar,
a teaspoon of honey.
See you in the morning!

Hops

Hops *(Humulus lupulus)*, a perennial, grows in northern temperate zones. Dark green, heart-shaped leaves grow on foot-long twining stalks. This herb requires deep, rich soil in an airy locale. The soil should be well worked and fertilized before planting. The plants may be trained to climb poles or screens, thus creating shade for the rest of the garden. When the leaves are picked and dried, they may be used to make a bedtime tea.

MARKET VALUE $10.45 per pound retail.

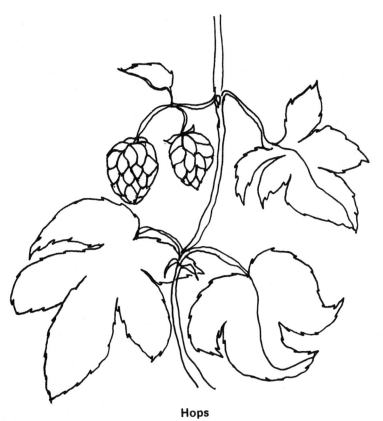

Hops

Coffee con Cordial

Goodies sometimes appear in disguise. The cordial
you drink with after-dinner coffee may contain an herb
from the backyard. Liqueurs are an elegant way to
enjoy herbs. You may use a single ingredient or mix
and match herbs with citrus. Rosemary, orris root,
wormwood, mint, angelica, and yarrow may be added
to liqueurs. The one I find most intriguing is made of
the common marigold.

Gather the flowers daily through July and refrigerate
until you've collected eight quarts. Then follow
these steps to transform them into liquid gold .
Combine marigolds with 1½ pounds of raisins. Set
aside;
Bring to a boil 7 pounds sugar, 2 pounds honey, and 3
gallons of water;
Strain and pour over the flower and raisin mix;
Cover tightly.
Let stand 24 hours. Stir once. Cover again.
Let stand another day.
Strain into a vat or barrel.
Add pared orange rind (no whites) and a pound of
sugar candy.
Add 4 to 5 tablespoons brewer's yeast.
Cover the bung hole of the keg. Fermentation will
become evident as a froth at the hole. When it
stops,
Add a pint of brandy and ½ ounce dissolved isinglass
(a translucent gelatin sometimes available at phar-
macies).
Cork vat and ignore for several months. Then serve to
make any occasion special.

Want to beat the high cost of coffee or avoid the
nerve-fraying effect of caffeine? Try making a coffee

substitute out of acorn shells, barley, chicory root, groundnut, peanut shells, chick-peas, rye, or soybeans.

Acorn

The acorn is a smooth, fat little nut with a beveled cap. Brown or green in color, it is found at the base of oak trees. Collect acorns in early fall. To prepare, boil dried nuts, wash several times in cold water and dry in the sun. Roast until crunchy; grind to a powder and use as you do coffee, sweetening with honey if desired.

You may mix one part acorn meal to four parts corn meal to make a tasty and nutritious "coffee" bread or pone.

Chicory

Wild endive or chicory (*Cichorium intybus*) is a commonly known coffee substitute. An herb to which the label "weed" aptly applies, the root, not the fruit, is what is used. Chicory has a stiff slender stem about three feet tall. It grows in any soil and bears sky-blue flowers that open by 7 A.M. and close at noon.

To collect, dig the root and wash, scrubbing with a brush. To prepare, slice root into long, thin strips. Tie five or six roots together or leave loose to dry in the oven, in direct sunlight, or in the attic. Roast and grind to a powder.

Chicory may be used as a coffee extender using one-half to three ounces of ground chicory to one pound of coffee. It will increase the yield of the pound by 10 cups.

MARKET VALUE $.60 to $2 per pound wholesale. Retail price is 10 cents for six ounces of ground chicory or a penny a tablet.

Chicory

Malt

A coffee substitute that is good for the whole family—no caffeine—is malt. It also may be used as a substitute for sugar.

Malt

Sprout a large quantity of wheat, rye, and barley.
Spread sprouts on a cookie sheet.
Bake at a low temperature for several hours until
    sprouts are dry and slightly brown.
Grind to a powder in a mill or blender.
Use as "instant" coffee substitute or as a sugar substi-
    tute on cereal or as a sweetener for baked goods.

Herbs Just for Fun

A synonym for fun is recreation. All herbs have some recreational quality, but some have more than others.

Let's skip marijuana and try tobacco substitutes.

Roll your own dried sunflower leaves or add a hint of mint to dried lettuce. You might also try corn silk, marjoram, raspberry leaves, rosemary, sage, and yerba santa. For a sweet, spicy or menthol tang, add lavender flowers, licorice root, allspice berries, or eucalyptus leaves. Lace your herbal smokes with dried catnip leaves, ginseng leaves, red poppyheads, wild lettuce, or yarrow blooms for a mildly euphoric effect.

Another use for roots and herbs is as a natural dye. Try tie-dyeing. The range of shades is subtle and earthy. You can control the intensity of color with careful attention to time. Remove the skein of wool or piece of cloth when it appears a shade darker than what you want; it will dry lighter. You can control fading by adding a mordant or fixative.

The results of your efforts will be determined by the plant condition, the soil quality, and the season of the year. Enjoy the surprises and experiment. Gather a favored herb and, instead of taking it as tea, tie-dye a cotton scarf or a skein of yarn. All plants have some coloring potential, but some are especially potent. Here is the primary color wheel of herbal dyes; discover the rest of the rainbow yourself.

For green: milkweed (ranges to orange with different mordants)
For yellow: chamomile flowers
For orange: onion peel
For blue: elder berries
For pink: safflower or St. John's wort.

Other herbs to try include sumac, goldenrod, wild carrot, and yarrow.

To preserve the color, add a mordant or fixative during a preliminary wash-soak process before dyeing. Some fixatives of old are hardwood ash, lye, sumac, and salt. More reliable and available, however, for use with wool is potassium alum, which may be bought in a pharmacy for under $2 a pint. Combine it in the following proportions with cream of tartar to make clear, bright, and shiny colors: 2/3 cup potassium alum to ¼ cup cream of tartar to dye a pound of yarn. To prepare, add alum and tartar to four or five gallons of warm water, stirring to dissolve. Add wet yarn and bring to a simmer on the stove. Turn off the heat and let the wool stand in the liquid overnight.

Now for the color. You may use fresh or dried plants as the season permits. Fresh plants yield brighter color, but dried work well, too. For winter projects store dried herbs in the freezer. Various parts of the plant may be used for dyeing just as for teas and tinctures. Gather the flowers from young plants just as they open—leaves at maturity, roots in the fall, berries at their ripest, and bark in the spring or fall. Dry well to avoid mildew.

Prepare the plant by chopping, pounding, and slightly pulverizing it. Tie into cheesecloth or an old nylon stocking, or release loose into the tepid water. Soak eight to 10 hours or longer.

Heat the dye water slowly to a near boil, meanwhile preparing the yarn to be dyed. Then, wet the yarn to be dyed in clear, hot water and immerse in dye solution. This is the best part of the coloring show. Poke—do not stir—the wool to make sure it is soaked through. Soak as long as it takes to achieve the color you want. When the wool looks a shade too dark, pull it out, rinse in water the same temperature as the dye water, and hang it up to dry. You may strain the dye water, saving the herbs for a second, weaker dye bath.

To dye cotton and linen, the process is slightly different. The mordant used to set the dye is tannic acid. It may be used alone or in combination with other fixatives mentioned before.

The material should be prewashed to remove the commercial sizing, which may interfere with the ability of the cloth to take the dye. Then, wet and wring out the material to be dyed.

To treat, dissolve 4 ounces of alum and 1 ounce of washing soda in 4 to 4½ gallons of water. Warm the water and stir in the material. Bring the water to a boil and keep it boiling for 1 hour. Turn off the heat and steep the material for 24 hours.

Next, steep the material in an astringent such as tannin. You may substitute 4 to 6 ounces of sumac leaves for the 1 ounce of tannin if it is not available. (Soak the leaves for one-half hour, boil for another half hour, and strain.)

Bring the material in tannin water to 140 to 160 degrees. Simmer for 1 hour; cool and allow to stand overnight. Rinse the material and add to another alum and washing soda bath in the proportions above. Soak the material overnight and squeeze it out in the morning. *Do not rinse.* Dry and store in a cool place. Rinse the mordant out just before dyeing.

There is coin in this realm of herb adventure, too—from raw herb to finished finery you can cash in. Collect or grow your own dye herbs and sell them to local yarn shops or area crafts people through stores that sell handmade products. If the yarn shop is willing, set up a Saturday demonstration to introduce customers to the potential of hand-dyed wools. Have pieces you have made yourself on hand for sale (as well as a variety of dyed yarns). Sell the herbs and give away the directions on how to use them.

Create your own scarves, dresses, shirts, and shawls, and introduce them into the line at the local apparel shop. Register for a summer crafts festival or street fair and sell your wares and services there, too. Take orders in the summer to keep yourself in business in the winter.

If you like to teach, contact a local learning exchange to register your talent, or call the local high school to offer to teach an adult education class. The possibilities are endless.

There are hundreds more herbs, each with distinct character, flavor, and uses. In the beginning you will be dazed by the possibilities. Take your time. Start with something familiar such as the day lily or Queen Anne's lace and get to know it better. Soon, you will move on to cousins and neighbors, perhaps finding your way to foraging or farming. Or you may just walk through a field with heightened awareness. Whatever level you reach in your acquaintance with herbs will be rewarding—from a nod of recognition to a place in your heart.

3

. . . For What Ails You

Sing O, Sing O, Sing O, Sing of Lydia Pinkham*
and her love, her love, her love
for the human race;
how she makes, she bottles, she sells
her vegetable compounds
and the pa-pers,
they publish her face.

—Win Stracke

It is required by unwritten law that every book on
herbs print a disclaimer regarding their medicinal
value. I tend to believe in them by intuition—
which perhaps in itself is a healing quality. And

*"Lydia Pinkham's" was the name of a product produced around the turn
of the century. You could not buy beer on Sunday, but you could buy Lydia
Pinkham, a compound containing 40 percent alcohol. Its purpose was to
heal ladies' ailments.

so must you, on your own behalf, lend credibility to the ancient and sustaining curative powers of plants. But, herewith, I make no promises that your ills will vanish with a dose of any herb listed. Three bits of advice I do lend you, however. Be cautious, be aware, and have faith. Also, beware how you promote the herbs you grow and sell yourself. Make suggestions not prescriptions or you leave yourself open for tar, feathers, and a lawsuit.

Hippocrates, the Greek physician whose oath of ethics is sworn by contemporary medical doctors, was an herbalist. And he is only one in a long line before and after his time who believed in the power of plants to cure.

American medicinal herb history began with the pioneers, who learned herbal lore from the Indians.

Indian medicine was not scientific in the Western sense of the word. It mixed myth, magic, and a religion of unity with the environment. The pioneers learned and adapted, and by 1787 had incorporated a list of 335 vegetable remedies.

Indians carried herbs in their medicine bags. And as the pioneers pushed west and resettled in each new place, the first garden to be planted was the herb garden, the frontier medicine chest. American folk medicine was born of a combination of Old Country wisdom and Indian lore. It is still practiced in the hills of Appalachia.

Herb gardening and gathering was a family affair until "Dr." Samuel Thompson made the first patent medicines. The medicine show, whose fast-talking salesmen preyed on the ill and desperate, followed.

Cures for diseases I'd rather not have

Plague, Fever or Horror—tormentilla
Blind Staggers—tansy
Gnawing of the Heart—spearmint
Green Wounds—knapweed
Insite to Venery—wild mint
Removing Proud Flesh—raspberry
Singing in the Ears—summer savory
Stinking Breath—rest harrow
Strange Sights and Fancies—bugle
Tartar—strawberry
Tetters—holy thistle
Wrinkles (premature)—oat groats
—*Proven Herbal Remedies*

Step right up!

The sucker born every minute met the charlatan with a gift for gab and a hot foot to get out of town. They were the audience and the hawker of the frontier medicine show.

"The most dramatic promotional stunt in the vending of alleged Indian remedies was the medicine show, which once ranked with the circus and the chautauqua as a seasonal relief to the monotony of small-town existence," writes Virgil J. Vogel in his book, *American Indian Medicine.**

Barkers touted *gen-u-ine* bottled native cures able to relieve all ills known to man, woman, or child—from loss of love to bunions. From 1700 to 1912, the main shows were those of the Oregon Indian Medicine Company, which was based in Pennsylvania, and the Kickapoo Indian Medicine Company, headquartered in New Haven, Connecticut.

Why were people so gullible? Well, those were simpler times, and the medicinal heritage of the pio-

*Reprinted by permission of University of Oklahoma Press.

neers was that of mystery and witchcraft. Perhaps they believed that disease came from having offended the gods, who had to be catered to through strange ceremonies and the intervention of exotic beings. The Indians were believed healthier for being in touch with the curing spirits.

As Americans became more sophisticated, and trained doctors became more available, the entertainment factor of the side show lessened, and an era ended.

With patent medicines came a greater demand for herbs, so herb growing as a cash crop developed.

The Shaker community in New Lebanon, New York, operated the first commercial herb farm. They planted 150 acres of "psychic gardens" that produced 4,000 pounds of herbs and roots sold to pharmaceutical companies in 1860 and 16,000 pounds per year in the following two decades.

"Why send to Europe's distant shores for plants which grow at our own doors?"
                    —From an old Shaker herb catalog

Today, the trend is to look backwards for a simpler way to heal. Modern drugs, some originally derived from herbal cures, have side effects that may often be worse than the illness they are prescribed to cure.

This chapter will provide a sample of some common complaints and recommended herbs for their relief. There are many plants assumed to have medicinal qualities, and more are being sought. One problem in writing about herbal medicine is that what is good for gout in New England may be better for blemishes in Oregon.

Herbs take longer than chemicals to relieve complaints—sometimes days or weeks longer. The idea is that the herb is working with your body to heal itself. So, be patient and the results will become evident with faithful dosing. Until we all become adept at healing ourselves, we should still depend on the medical profession when their attention is warranted. Do not let a condition go untreated for any length of time. When in doubt, see a doctor. For expert advice on herbal healing, consult a homeopath or naturopath, usually found in or near large metropolitan areas. (See Chapter 10 for a talk with one such physician).

Sorry, you can't have it both ways.
If you're taking a drug for an ailment you shouldn't start an herbal cure.

This book can cover only a few of the hundreds of plants whose qualities lend themselves to human cure. However, any plant whose botanical name contains the word "officinale" or common name contains the word "wort" or "bane" can be counted on to cure.

Language is often the first stumbling block in any new pursuit. The following is a glossary of basic terms to aid the herbal curer.

Creams and ointments—Cook 1 ounce of finely crushed herb in ¾ pound of lard. Strain fat and add to it some melted beeswax. Reheat slowly to blend and cool. Or, pound 1 part fresh or dried herb into 2 parts cold cream or petroleum jelly.

Decoction—Combine in a porcelain or glass pot ½ ounce of dried root and 1 pint of water. Simmer 20 minutes to reduce water to half. Strain and store in a cool, dark place. This stays fresh longer than the other mixtures. The recommended dose is 1 cup daily.

Infusion—This is the commonest way to take herbal medicine. Pour 1 pint of boiling water over 1 ounce of dried herb (3 handfuls fresh). Set aside for 3 to 4 hours. Or, bring 1 ounce of herb and 1 pint of cold water to a boil and simmer up to 2 minutes. Set aside 3 hours. When properly stored in a cool, dark place, this remedy will stay fresh and useful up to 4 days. Recommended daily dosage: 2 to 3 wineglassfuls.

Juices—Using a juicer or a mortar and pestle, extract the juices from the leaves and fresh stalks of the chosen herb. Add a little sugar to make the herb juice palatable. (When preparing roots, add a little white wine and the bruising will be easier.) If the fresh juice is too harsh to be taken directly, allow it to settle and take when it is clear.

Oils—Put 2 tablespoons of finely crushed herb in a jar. Fill ¾ full with pure vegetable oil. Add 1 tablespoon plain vinegar. Cover and store in hot sunlight for 3 weeks before using. To enrich, strain oil after first and second weeks, adding fresh herbs each time.

Poultice—An external treatment, the poultice is said to draw poisons from the body and induce healing. There are two methods for making poultices. Either soften the herbs in just enough warm water to cause separation into soft flakes (or, using ground herb, add enough water to make a paste). Apply to the affected area with a tight bandage. Or—the alternate method—use a standard infusion. Slowly add just enough corn flour (cornstarch) to make a thin paste, stirring constantly. Spread this paste warm on a clean bandage and apply to the affected area. Use the poultice only once; do not rewarm. Replace with a warm poultice when the first cools. Useful poultice herbs are comfrey, poppy, violet, St. John's wort, and adder's tongue. Such treatments are good for swollen glands in the neck, groin, and prostate and for boils, eruptions, and abesses.

Syrup—To 1 pint boiling water add 3 pounds of brown sugar (or malt or honey or corn syrup). Boil until thick and add herbs. Refrigerate.

Tincture—Add 3 ounces of powdered herb to a quart of low-odor medicinal alcohol. Store in an airtight container in a warm place for 3 weeks. Shake daily.

Tisane—Use the same method as for an infusion but alter the quantity to 1 teaspoon of dried herb (3 of fresh) to 1 cup of water, and brew the mixture only three to five minutes.

If Nicholas Culpeper, the noted herbalist of the 17th century, were alive today, he would cast your horoscope before recommending a concoction to cure your ill. Astrology and herbs were linked during the renaissance: It was believed that the stars ruled the events in people's lives and that each astrological sign affected a specific part of the body. Since individual herbs affected corresponding body parts, astrology and herbalism became partners in attempts to cure.

I offer the following list of herbs as basic for any "natural" medicine cabinet. Choose what you care to have on hand according to your most common ailments.

Comfrey (Symphytum officinale), Healing Herb, Knit Bone.

This aspirin of the herb world grows well wild and is gaining ground as a popular and profitable crop. It is a hardy perennial, growing up to 3 feet in height with a thick, spindle-shaped root and a rough and hairy stem. It is stout and angular and has 10 inch lower leaves decreasing in size as they grow up the stem. It may have either creamy yellow or blue-purple flowers on a scorpion-tail stem.

Comfrey

Comfrey enjoys a long season—from April or May to the first frost—and may even thrive longer; the root can survive at up to 40 degrees (F) below zero. Harvesting can be done every 10 to 30 days during the season, each harvest being taken just before blooms appear, when the plant is 12 to 18 inches high. Leaves should be cut with a knife at the end of the day when they are rich with nutrients, allowing a 2-inch stump to grow again.

Comfrey contains calcium, potassium, phosphorus, and vitamins A and C. It is also the only land plant that contains vitamin B^{12}.

Almost a cureall, comfrey is good for coughs and colds and for knitting bones. As a hot poultice it soothes arthritic joints or swollen tonsils. It is nature's "preparation H." It helps to heal burns and bruises, cure kidney stones, deactivate tuberculosis, and remove wrinkles. Raw leaves may be taken for an ulcer, and tea for lung troubles. Comfrey cream renews aging skin and clears up acne.

Comfrey lends itself well to a small herb farm operation. It may be raised from purchased plants, top cuttings, or root cuttings—the last is the cheapest way to buy and sell through the mail.

MARKET VALUE $5.60 per pound retail for leaves.
$4.98 per pound retail for roots.
$5.94 per pound retail for powder.

Catnip (Nepeta catoria), Catnep, Catmint.

And you thought this was only for your furry friend curled up in the rocker. Catnip thrives in New England and other parts of the U.S. A three-foot high wild perennial related to the mints, it has gray, "furred," heart-shaped leaves. Its flowers are dense pink to lavender whorls on short stalks and bloom from July through September.

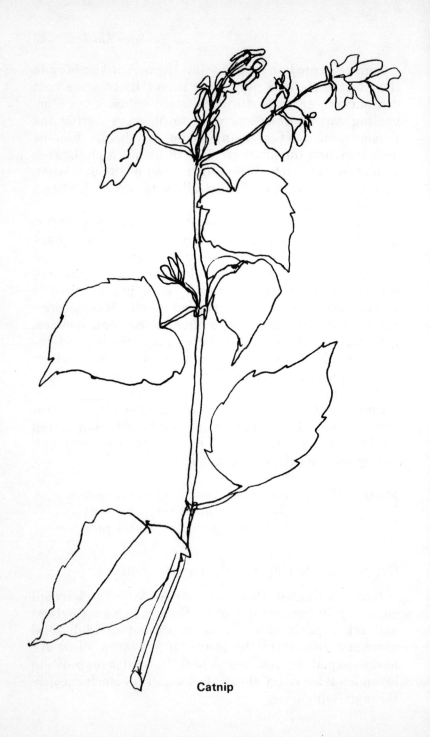

Catnip

Sow the seed directly into the rich soil of your garden in late April or early May. Set 18 inches apart and leave the plants alone as they grow. If you bruise the leaves to release their odor, the crop will belong to the cat.

Harvest the flower tops when they are in full bloom in August, before the yellowing of the leaves sets in, or take the whole plant, strip it of its leaves, and dry them in the shade for two to three days.

Now is the time to share with the cat of your choice. Stuff a felt toy with the weed, or simply crumble a handful on the floor. The rest you can use for yourself as a mild stimulant and anti-spasmodic to alleviate nervous headaches, hysteria and nightmares, colic, and the kind of "insanity" to which we are all prone on occasion.

Prepare as tea sweetened with honey or flavored with lemon. It's a hot weather refreshment and a winter cold cure. As an infusion, adult dosage is two to three tablespoons; child's dosage, two to three teaspoons.

Catnip is also a rat repellent. It figures.

MARKET VALUE $.90 per pound retail.

Coltsfoot (Tussilago farfara), Cough Wort, Hall Foot, Ass's Foot.

This native American plant flourishes in damp, clay soil in full sunlight. It is recognized by its bright yellow flowers, which appear before its long-stemmed serrated leaves that are shaped like horses' hooves. Wooly, like a colt at first, the leaves smooth with age.

Coltsfoot contains calcium, potassium, sulfur, vitamin C, mucilage (a natural adhesive), and tannin (used as an astringent and styptic). For tonic tea and cough medicine, a decoction of 1 ounce of leaves added

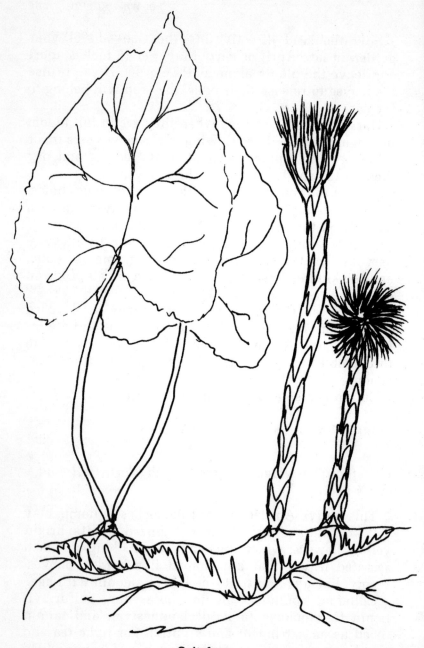

Coltsfoot

to 1 quart of water (boiled down to a pint) is sweetened with honey and recommended for coughs and asthma. A dose of one teacup is suggested.

MARKET VALUE $7.68 per pound retail.

The British herb tobacco recommended for lung trouble: coltsfoot leaves, buckbean, eyebright, betony, rosemary, thyme, lavender and chamomile flowers.

Dandelion (Taraxacum officinale), Lion's Tooth, Swine Snout, Puffball.

By whatever name, this well-known weed thrives in good soil in grassy open places and fields. Its roots reach deep and sometimes are branched. Bright green, saw-toothed leaves and hollow stems are crowned by broad yellow heads.

Although they flourish in residential lawns and gardens, do not dig dandelions if you have applied weed killer to the grass. Dig the roots of wild plants either in early spring or fall. Cultivating dandelions ensures large roots and grants a yield of four to five tons of fresh roots to a cultivated acre. (The shrinkage is great, however—100 units diminish to 22 when dried). Separate the root cleanly from its leaf base for the best quality. Dry for two weeks, until the roots snap clean and are white on the inside.

Dandelions contain vitamins A, B, and C, and are largely used as a remedy for liver and kidney complaints, rheumatism, and skin eruptions. The juices are believed to remove warts and corns.

New, spring greens may be blanched and used in a fresh salad. Their natural nutritive salts are said to purify the blood and destroy acids.

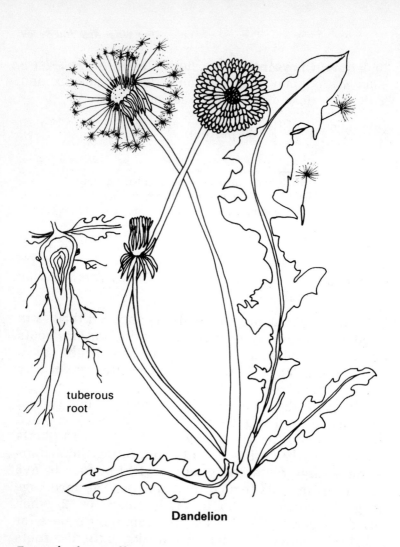

Dandelion

Remedy for Gallstones

1 ounce each: dandelion roots, parsley root, balm root;
½ ounce each: ginger root and licorice root. Place
in 2 quarts of water, gently simmer to half and
strain. Drink a wineglassful every two hours.
Take as a tea for hypochondria.

MARKET VALUE $5.12 per pound retail for leaves.
$4.95 per pound retail for roots.

Feverfew (Chrysanthemum parthenium), Bachelor's Buttons

Once considered a cleanser of sickroom atmosphere, this member of the daisy family grows wild and free in open fields. As a cultivated crop it needs little attention after being planted in April or autumn in well-drained, well-nourished soil. (Sow seeds in February or March and thin to two to three inches apart. Transplant on a rainy June day leaving one foot between plants and two feet between rows.)

Feverfew grows to two to three feet and bears gold-green leaves and daisy-like blooms with one-inch-wide yellow centers. Its healing qualities, transmitted by an

Feverfew

infusion of flowers, include reducing sensitivity to pain. using the whole plant, it has been found to have strong healing powers. Mixed with honey, it is said to ease coughing, wheezing, and breathing difficulties. A tincture of feverfew mixed with a half-pint of cold water and applied externally keeps gnats, mosquitoes, and bees away from the body. For the nerves, mix feverfew with wine and nutmeg. Gather feverfew at the peak of its maturity, with the left hand, speaking the name of the fever victim aloud, never looking behind you!

MARKET VALUE $12 per pound retail.

Goldenseal (Hydrastis canadenis)—A Universal Cure

This is a powerful plant drug and it should command the highest respect. Small in size, goldenseal grows from a yellow root to about six inches high. It contains a single main leaf and two secondary ones. Its single flower is erect and small, with greenish-white sepals; its crimson berries ripen in July.

Found in the rich, well-drained, forested hill country east of the Mississippi, goldenseal is gathered in the fall for its rhizome and root. The Cherokees mixed the herb with bear's grease for an insect repellent. Other Indian tribes used it as a body paint and to color their clothing yellow.

As a remedy, goldenseal is said to be powerful medicine for ailments of the nasal mucous membranes, the gastrointestinal tract, vagina, and uterus, and the urethra. Combined with cayenne, it is reported to be a remedy for advanced alcoholism.

Goldenseal was listed as a medicinal plant by 1850, but it no longer is on the official drug charts. Its properties remain on the best-seller list with herbalists, however.

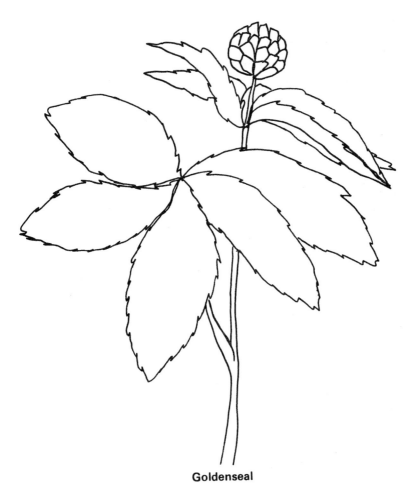

Goldenseal

As a profit crop for cultivation, one should think twice about goldenseal. As sensitive as ginseng, goldenseal needs well-drained soil that is rich in humus and a locale that is 60 to 70 percent shaded. The U.S. Department of Agriculture recommends planting from roots, cultivating the plants for two years, then harvesting for market. The rhizome deteriorates after the fourth year. Like ginseng, however, goldenseal has an international following and promises a sizeable return on the investment.

Two Goldenseal Cures

Use in lotion form for treating eye inflammations and for general cleansing.

Make an infusion. Take for habitual constipation, loss of appetite, and vomiting.

MARKET VALUE $8 to $16 per pound wholesale.
$36 per pound retail.

Juniper (Juniperus communis)

The berries of this small-to-medium-sized evergreen tree or shrub are used in the manufacture of gin.

Junipers grow well in dry, sandy, or gravelly soil in exposed locations. This hardy plant bears gray-green or blue-green needlelike leaves. The berries, used in medicine, are blue and ripen in two years.

Because the seeds take two to three years to germinate, junipers are best started using the top four to six inches of an established shrub. Cut the tip in August and strip it of its needles up one inch from the new base. Plant in a cold frame bed of sand five inches deep. Water, cover with a glass, and keep shaded. Transplant outside the following summer.

An old symbol of protection, juniper shoots may be burned to disinfect a sick room. The berries can be strung as beads or used for dye. Prepare an infusion of berries by soaking three tablespoons of berries in water to cover. Then add the soaked berries to a pot of boiling water. Allow this combination to stand for half an hour. The infusion may be taken four times a day for stimulation of appetite and digestion, kidneys, and bladder. A strong tea makes a good cleanser for snake, insect, and dog bites. The tea of the root is said to control venereal disease. It is also claimed to increase sexual prowess, ease leprosy, and improve the mind.

Juniper should not be taken when neuritis is present.

MARKET VALUE $4.48 per pound retail.

Juniper

Marshmallow (Althaea officinalis)

Found in damp meadows and salty marshes of warm climates, marshmallow root gets its Latin name from the Greek *altho,* which means *cure.* It grows to three or four feet and has a roundish velvety stem and two- to three-inch-long leaves. Pale, bluish flowers bloom in August and September and are followed by flat, round fruit called "cheeses."

Introduced by the Romans into England, marshmallow starts easily from seed in the spring. Plants should

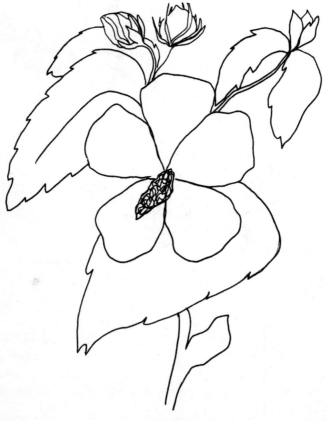

Marshmallow

be two feet apart in any soil in sun or shade. However, for best results plant in the moist ground beside a running brook.

Leaves should be harvested in August, just as the flowers begin to bloom. To catch them at their peak, they should be gathered early in the morning. The root may be dug later and dried, crushed, or powdered.

Marshmallow is said to have the power to soothe bruises, sprains, and muscle aches and to ease inflammation in the urinary tract, respiratory organs, and the alimentary canal. Boiled in wine instead of water, it makes a mighty cure for coughs, bronchitis, and other chest ailments. For a decoction, take 5 pints of water and ¼ pound of dried root, boil down to 3 pints, and strain. It may be used as an eyewash or a sitz bath to soften the skin.

Marshmallow lozenges

Mix 1½ ounces powdered root with 4½ ounces brown sugar and enough mucilage of gum tragacanth to hold together in lozenge form.

MARKET VALUE $5.76 per pound retail.

Mullein (Verbascum thapsus), Woolen Blanket Herb, Flannel Flower.

Mullein is a naturalized weed from the East that spread west rapidly. It grows well in poor soil, giving forth a thick profusion of woolly leaves. In the second year, a tall, yellow flower-studded stem rises four to eight feet. A plant steeped in mystic reputation, mullein down is said to have been used as wicks for witches' candles.

Although it abounds wild in the U.S., it is also easy

Mullein

to cultivate. The only attention it needs once sown is to be free from competing weeds.

Medicinally, both the flowers and leaves are used. The leaves are dried, flaked, and used as "tobacco" for congested throats. An infusion of one ounce dried powdered leaves to one pint of milk is a treatment for coughs, constipation—or diarrhea. (Mullein demonstrates one of herbs' curiosities—that a single potion may act as cure for completely opposite complaints.) Strain the mixture (to remove the rough hairs), add one teaspoon of honey, and serve warm by the wineglassful for the above complaints.

The flowers may be steeped in olive oil to make an ointment for frostbite, hemorrhoids, and earache.

MARKET VALUE $10.24 retail for flowers.
                $7.68 retail for leaves.

Peppermint (Mentha piperita)

It is the taste that gets you first, a refreshing coolness that has been captured by gum and candy companies for years. But peppermint and its sibling mints have other qualities, too.

Peppermint grows pointed oval leaves growing opposite each other on a purple-green square stem. In late spring, it sprouts tiny violet flowers. Peppermint grows fast and furiously in moist, rich soil commonly known as muck. Michigan and Indiana have large areas of peppermint, as do Wisconsin, Oregon, and Washington. And recently some reclaimed land in Louisiana has been put into peppermint cultivation. It is estimated that more than 45,000 acres of land are devoted to this easily cultivated and refreshing weed. It is the world's most popular herb.

Peppermint is the lazy herb farmer's friend. All that needs to be done is to keep it free of weeds during the

Peppermint

summer. One or two plants started in fertile, moist soil will yield a good bed in a season. For larger farm cultivation the practice is to dig runners in the early spring and place them in shallow trenches.

Peppermint may be harvested three times a year to within an inch of the ground. This is done when the lower leaves have begun to yellow. The leaves are stripped from the stems and dried whole in warm shade. The bed should then be covered for the winter with two inches of rich compost.

Besides being a flavor enhancer for less palatable potions and an additive to such teas as alfalfa, clover flower, chamomile, licorice, strawberry, and raspberry leaf, peppermint is also used as a pleasant healing drug.

For colds and flu—infuse peppermint and elder flowers (with or without boneset or yarrow). Drink freely.
For stomach cramps—mix peppermint with milk.
For relief of gas—take one to two drops of extract in a half glass of water.
For insomnia—take an infusion of two parts peppermint, to one part rue and one part wood betony.
In general—peppermint is used as a stimulant, stomachic, and carminative expectorant.

MARKET VALUE $5 to $8 per pound retail.

Potentilla (Potentilla), Five-finger Grass

This is a hill-country herb grown in the Ozarks, Arkansas, Kentucky, and Tennessee. Found in meadows and open fields of hillsides, this sprawling wayside weed looks like wild strawberry. It is a hardy herb related to roses and grows from two to eighteen inches tall in sandy soil and sunny locations.

One species of potentilla is silvery cinquefoil, which

grows from five to twelve inches tall and sprouts small yellow flowers in clusters. Its leaves are fern-like, dark green on top and silvery wool underneath. It blooms from May through September.

Potentilla, besides being used as a tea, can also be used as an astringent, a mouthwash, lotion for diarrhea, piles, and sore throat. It is also handy for washing cuts and abrasions. The root of the potentilla is a natural red dye.

MARKET VALUE $6.54 per pound retail.

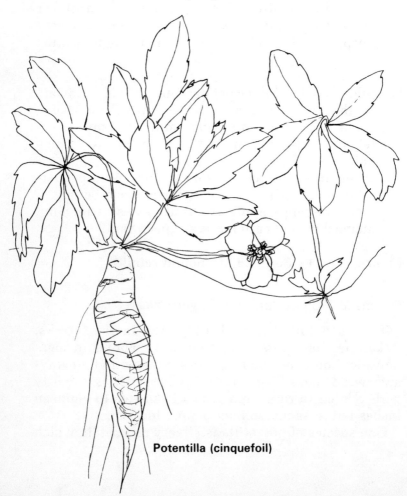

Potentilla (cinquefoil)

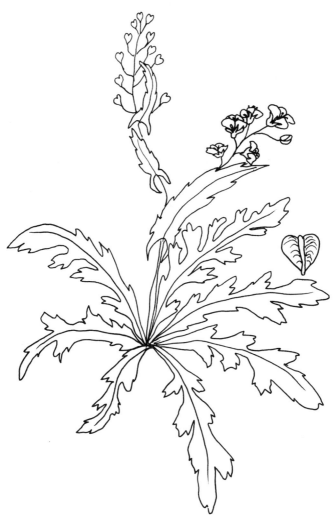

Shepherd's purse

Shepherd's Purse (Capsella Bursa-pastoris)

The English call it pepper and salt, pick-pocket, and shepherd's sprout. This curiously named herb is an international weed. Flourishing in mediocre soil, it grows to two feet in rich soil and sports two- to six-inch-long green, hairy leaves in irregular form. The plant has slender stem with a few branches containing small, unassuming white flowers. The plant's fruit is shaped like a piece of pie that separates into two boat-shaped halves containing yellow seeds.

The entire plant is used to stop profuse bleeding, both internal and external (it contains vitamins C and K, which aid clotting). Shepherd's purse also increases the flow of urine when infection is present and helps relieve children's bed wetting problems. An infusion of 12 ounces of water and 1 ounce of the herb, boiled down to a cup, strained, and administered cold, should do the trick.

MARKET VALUE $4 per pound retail.

Solomon's Seal (Polygonatum multiflorum)

Graceful round stems with broad oval leaves rise from 18 to 24 inches from this knotted, creeping root herb. At the axils of the leaves, waxy white and yellow-green flowers droop in clusters of two to seven.

Solomon's seal is a woodland herb, a hardy plant that prefers light soil and shade. To cultivate, sow seeds in autumn for a spring crop, or divide the root. The root of this plant is dug in the fall, dried, ground and used as an astringent, demulcent, and tonic. An infusion of 1 ounce of herb to a pint of boiling water and taken by the wineglassful is suggested for bleeding lungs and for menstrual problems. The T-bone steak of the vegetable world, Solomon's seal makes a nice poultice for a black eye, too:

Combine bruised root and cream;
Lay it on the shiner.

The healing and restorative qualities of this herb are still being explored.

MARKET VALUE $31.20 per pound retail.

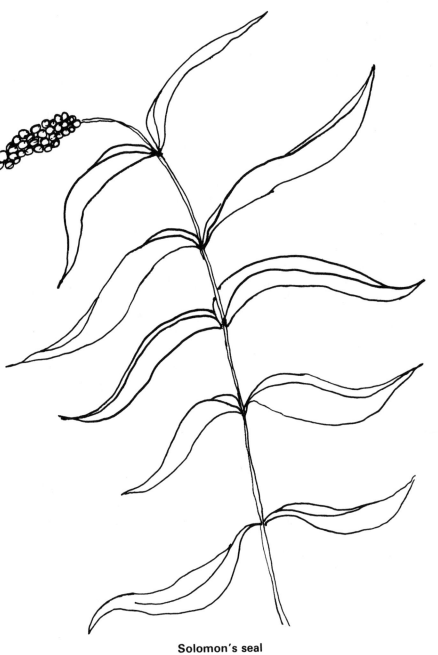

Solomon's seal

Valerian (Valeriana officinalis), Garden Heliotrope, Lady's Slipper, All-heal, and Phu. (A reference to its smell)

Like several other herbs, valerian stands out from the rest for its qualities in relieving many human discomforts. This dark green plant, which grows to three to five feet, is a powerful nerve stimulant, antispasmodic, sedative, and painkiller. Extract of valerian is used to treat epilepsy, and it is an antidote for insomnia, migraine headaches, and other diseases of the nervous system. With the cure comes a caution. Valerian should be ingested only in small doses then very infrequently.

Valerian grows across the U.S. in nearly any soil. It requires regular watering and full sun, and in return produces small bunches of peculiarly fragrant flowers in lavender, pink, or white from June to September. In the garden it attracts earthworms, and a spray containing valerian used on other plants once a month during the summer will strengthen them. A cultivated crop is best started by transplanting the wild plants and taming them in your garden. If that is not possible, sow seeds inside in March or outside in April. Thin every three years, leaving a foot of space between plants.

Because the power of this medicinal plant is in its rhizome, it is advised that you cut off the flower heads as they appear, to improve the underground growth. Harvest the rhizomes in September or October, before the frost. Wash thoroughly and dry at 120 degrees (F) until they are brittle. Then store in a dry place.

Again, this is a powerful drug.

MARKET VALUE $7 per pound retail.

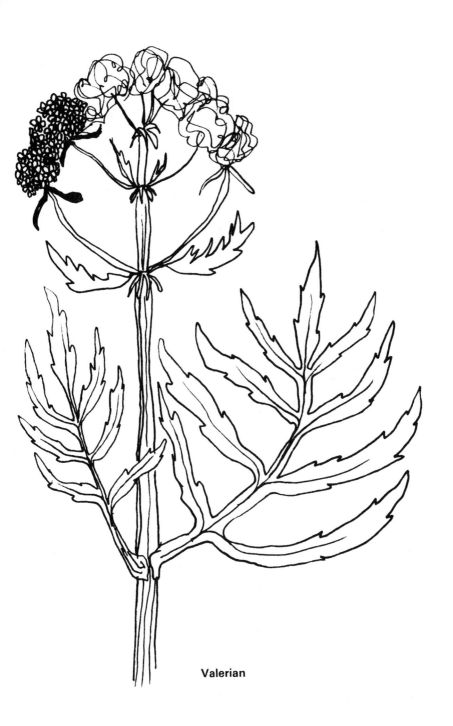

Valerian

Yarrow

Yarrow (Achillea millefolium), Nosebleed Weed, Sneezewort, Bloodwort.

Once known in a knight's first-aid kit, this versatile herb has many a moniker—old man's pepper, soldier's woundwort, and devil's plaything to name a few more. It is the beverage of Swiss mountaineers, and is said to be good for colds and fevers.

It is a naturalized American plant growing wild in any kind of soil. Found mostly in the eastern part of the U.S., it springs up along roadsides and in old fields in blooms of white, red, orange, or yellow. (The white and red are the variety used for medicinal purposes; the yellow and orange lend themselves to lovely dried weed arrangements.) Three- to four-inch-long leaves grow alternately at the base of a long, rough stem. The flowers bloom from June to September. The entire herb is collected for use in August.

Start your own yarrow from seed or by root division in light, sandy soil, keeping the plantings evenly moist until germination takes place. Or start them indoors in March.

To prepare, chop the leaves and stems and dry at 90 to 100 degrees (F). Use as an astringent, tonic, and stimulant. An infusion of 1 ounce yarrow and 1 pint boiling water plus 1 teaspoon of honey and 3 drops of Tabasco sauce is said to cure the worst of colds. Wrap the patient in blankets; the combination causes heavy sweating. Or, you may use elder flowers and peppermint instead of honey and tabasco.

Yarrow also makes a bracing winter tea; its wet leaves placed on the brow are said to relieve a headache. And, depending on whether or not you have a nosebleed, yarrow is said to start or to stop it. (A bleeding nose will ease a headache, if you wonder why anyone might *want* a bloody nose).

MARKET VALUE $5.12 per pound retail.

Yellow dock

Yellow dock (Rumex crispus)

Also known as *curly dock,* this is one of a variety of docks, and it's the big brother of the lot. Found growing with many other herbs—in the waysides and waste places of the countryside—dock grows to about 3 feet tall with six to ten lancelike curly edged leaves. The greenish flowers that bloom in June and July are tiny and packed in whorls along the stem, making the stem appear more fuzzy than floral. Reddish seeds follow and remain throughout the winter. Collect the roots in late summer and early autumn, and split, dry, and store them for later use.

A true tonic, yellow dock is believed to clean the blood and by so doing clear the skin, since outward eruptions are said to be evidence of blood impurities. The herb is also used to aid digestion and as a mild laxative. As an ointment it relieves itching of the skin. To make ointment, boil root in vinegar and mix the soft pulp with petroleum jelly.

MARKET VALUE $9.94 per pound retail.

Four for women

Many of the medicinal herbs have special qualities that are said to improve the health of women. The following four have been selected for their general qualities and for those that affect women's systems.

Balm (Melissa officinalis), Sweet Balm, Lemon Balm.

A cultivated American crop, this small tree bears pungent, lemon-smelling leaves that grow opposite one another on the stem. Their broad oval shape lends a backdrop to pale yellow flowers between June and October. Balm grows well from seed in healthy, well-fed soil with plenty of water and sunshine. The herb needs freedom from weeds and an occasional loosening of the dirt around the roots.

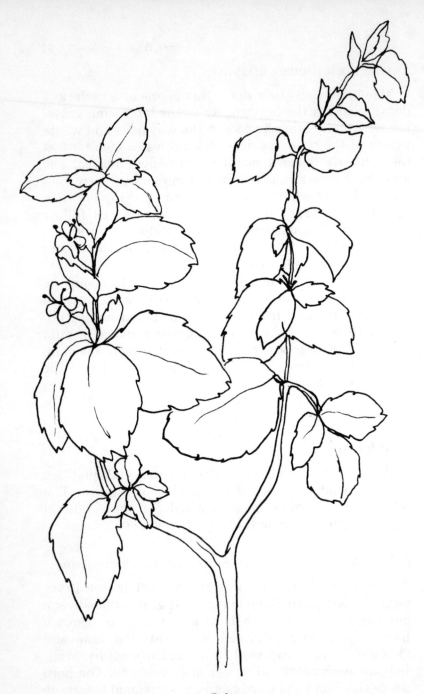

Balm

Harvest the leaves and plant tops for use fresh or dry. To prepare tea, pour 1 pint of boiling water over 1 ounce of balm, infusing for 15 minutes. Cool and strain. Drink as often as you like. If you wish to, you may add a sweetener and a little lemon for a cooling summer refresher.

Balm rhymes with calm and is synonymous with *ease* in my vocabulary. It soothes overworked brains, is a mouthwash for aching teeth, and relieves headache. It is said to reduce menstrual pain, to make the heart merry, and to drive out melancholy. As a poultice, it may be applied to boils and insect bites to ease their itch and sting. Balm also attracts bees.

MARKET VALUE $7.60 per pound retail.

Witch Hazel (Hamamelis virginiana)

Hazel wood conjures up water in the form of a divining rod; hence, the name. The extract of this eastern U.S. herb sells by the barrels and barrels.

This perennial tree or shrub is a vigorous herb that is known for its crooked trunk. The leaves drop off in the autumn, at which time it blooms. Pale yellow flowers with thin petals glow throughout the winter months, from October into the spring. The seeds mature the following summer.

The leaves, three to five inches long, are medicinal. The bark is also used for treatment in cases calling for a sedative, and it is said to be a treatment and pain killer for piles, bruises, swellings, diarrhea, and mucous discharge. An infusion is said to ease sore throat, gums, and teeth.

A witch hazel douche is said to clear up vaginitis. A decoction may be taken for weakness after an abortion. And an application of witch hazel to an erupted varicose vein is said to stop the bleeding.

This amazing herb goes to work on bites and stings

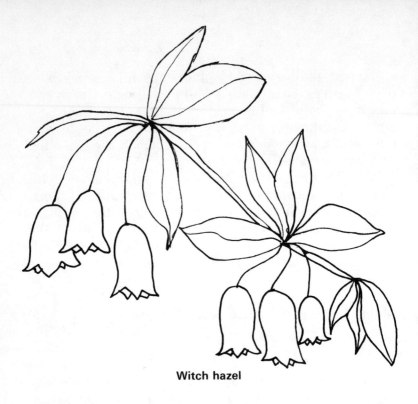

Witch hazel

of insects, sunburn, scalds, and burns. As an astringent, it makes a bracing aftershave lotion and gargle, and it even recharges the tired muscles of athletes. It can be used as an after-shampoo rinse, a refresher for tired feet, and a wash to stop the itch of poison ivy.

To make an extract of witch hazel:

Immerse 1 ounce of witch hazel leaves and twigs in 2 cups of alcohol;
Let stand 2 weeks, shaking daily;
Strain;
Use full strength on bruises and insect bites, burns, and skin inflammations or diluted in warm water for eyelid inflammation. Or make an ointment (1- to 9-ratio) for local application.

MARKET VALUE $6 per pound retail for leaves and bark.

Tansy (Tanacetum vulgare), Bitter Buttons, Stinking Willie.

The names are deceiving. This herb is said to pack a mighty punch against frayed nerves, indigestion, sprains, pimples, and weakened kidneys. The Catawba Indians used it in a steambath for sore and swollen feet and ankles.

Tansy is a strong-willed perennial that tends to dominate any open spaces it grows in. Perferring chalky soil, it grows from two to three feet tall and has

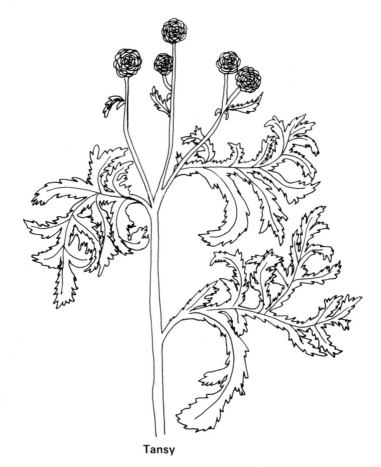

Tansy

six-inch-long and four-inch-wide fernlike leaves. Its flat-headed yellow flowers appear late in the warm weather. To keep this herb from taking over, it can be planted in a sunken drum in moderately fertile soil.

Harvest tansy at its peak, before the leaves have started to yellow. Strip the leaves from the young plants and dry at 90 degrees (F) in the shade.

Several books credit tansy with culinary qualities. It may be substituted for nutmeg and cinnamon as a flavoring, or it may be used sparingly in salad dressings and omelets. But, considering its narcotic powers, tansy might best be handled with care, especially by women.

Tansy, rubbed on the body, is said to increase fertility and, when taken internally, is said to cause abortion. It is also purported to stimulate and promote menstruation. Tansy can be taken as a tonic or a tea. Tansy by the back door discourages the invasion of flies, mosquitoes, and ants into the house. It also can be used as a red dye.

MARKET VALUE $2.50 per pound retail.

Wild Cherry (Prunus virginiana)

Wild cherry, a delightful herbal tea, is said to be second only to sassafras as a home remedy. It grows as a full-fledged tree in the northern, southwestern, and central United States, to 50 to 80 feet tall and two to four feet in diameter. Fortunately, it is not the leaves you want, but the root bark.

To recognize this herb, look for three- to five-inch-long leaves growing on petioles with two pairs of red glands. White flowers bloom in May, and purplish, pea-shaped fruit ripens in late summer or early fall.

Collect the root bark fresh each year; dry, powder

Wild cherry

and use as an astringent, tonic, pectoral (treating diseases of the chest) or sedative. Wild cherry may be used as a treatment for bronchitis, catarrh, consumption, nervous coughing, and whooping cough. Southern mountaineers take the tea to treat measles; Cherokee women took a warm infusion of the herb at the onset of labor.

MARKET VALUE $4.80 per pound retail.

Other herbs

Other herbs whose qualities lend themselves to women's complaints are

Comfrey—a douche; and a leaf compress eases the pain of swollen breasts. It is said to increase the sexual appetite.
Feverfew—strong healing power for women; if boiled and drunk in white wine, is said to strengthen the womb.
Goldenseal—a tonic for morning sickness.
Marshmallow root—a douche.
Plantain—cures a multitude of women's complaints; drink daily to increase fertility.

A douche recipe

Mix ½ cup each of peppermint, spearmint, comfrey, and myrtle leaves;
Steep ½ cup of the mixture in 2 cups boiling water for 15 minutes.
Cool;
Strain and use.

Two from the great outdoors

Two herbs will appeal to campers, hikers, fisherfolk, and hunters.

Boneset

Boneset (Eupatorian perfoliatum) makes a bitter tea that the Iroquois used as a fever remedy and the plantation blacks used as a tonic. During the Civil War, boneset was considered a substitute for quinine.

Also known as *thoroughwort,* which implies its versatility, boneset is recognized in the United States

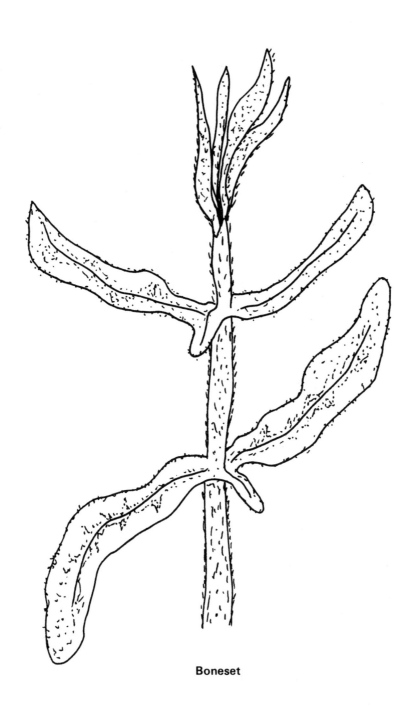

Boneset

Pharmacopeia, the official compendium of pharmaceuticals in the U.S. It is a two-to-four-foot perennial that grows wild in low, damp meadows throughout the country. Its round, downy stem branches at the top with flower stems hosting 10 to 20 white flowerets from July to September. Its leaves grow further down on the stem opposite one another, creating a collarlike formation.

The entire herb may be collected for use and be made into an infusion of 1 ounce of dried herb to 1 pint of boiling water. This may be taken hot as a cure or cold as a tonic by the wineglassful. The warm infusion is best taken by outdoor people as a shield against the general cold. Homebodies may take boneset as a stimulant, febrifuge (cool drink to reduce fever), or laxative.

MARKET VALUE $4 per pound retail.

Labrador Tea (Ledum latifolium), St. James' Tea, Rosemary Flowers, Marsh Tea, Moth Herb.

A native American tea, this shrub grows in far northern United States and in Nova Scotia and Hudson's Bay as a four- to five-foot evergreen with irregular and woolly branches. Five-petaled flowers grow in clusters and bloom in June and July. During the American Revolution the leaves of this plant, found only in cold bogs and wooded hills, were used for tea to diminish the effects of the cold winter. Labrador tea works as a tonic, a diaphoretic (perspiration producer), and a pectoral. Its camphor-like smell makes it pleasant and soothing to use while curing the body of cold, fever, infection, or itch. An infusion of two to four ounces taken three to four times a day is said to effect a cure. A strong decoction may also be used as a wash to kill lice or other outdoor hitchhikers known to backpackers.

Caution is suggested in ingesting this tea: An overdose produces intoxication.

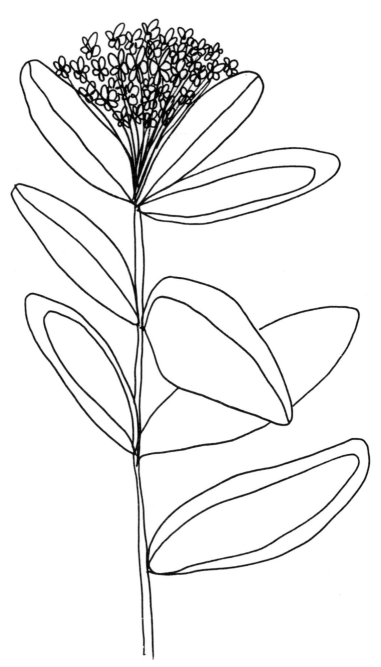

Labrador tea

Your herbal medicine chest

Some of the herbal remedies indicated here must be made on the spot when the affliction occurs. You may keep a quantity of herbs in dry form ready for such an occasion. Bottle the herbs in small, tightly lidded jars—the kind you find containing culinary herbs and spices in the grocery store. Be sure to label with correct popular and botanical name, date herb was put up so you will know when its potency has diminished, directions for preparation, and dosage.

If there's not enough room on the label, make up a chart similar to the one which follows and keep it handy. You might also include in the chart the general directions for making infusions, poultices, and so on that appear at the beginning of this chapter.

That, and a copy of a complete medical herbal will start you on the road to home health care, the natural way.

Cold and flu—½ ounce each of yarrow, peppermint, elder flowers, and 6 chili peppers.

Headache—½ ounce each of rosemary, thyme, wild thyme, wild marjoram, peppermint, lavender flowers, rose flowers, and marjoram. Prepare as an infusion as needed.

Gas—½ ounce each of aniseed, fennel, caraway, coriander.

Flu—elder flowers and peppermint tea.

Deodorant—lovage tea.

Hiccoughs—dill weed seed tea.

Summary

In this chapter I have introduced you to a few herbs you might begin collecting or growing to replace the common drugs in your medicine chest. Take a good look behind the mirror. How old are the pills and powders? Do you know what they contain?

Now, take a look in the mirror. Are you as healthy as you would like to be? Perhaps herbs could help. Add some natural cures to the cabinet shelf.

"Self-healing strengthens the will."
—Hazrat Inayat Khan

Shakers to Sufis through herbs

A spiritual community of about 100 people are reviving the Shaker herb farm in New Lebanon, New York. The "abode of the message" is the headquarters for the Sufi order in the West—a community of people who seek the "source" through "love, harmony and beauty."

On a quarter acre of land, from stock gathered from two of the remaining Shaker communities—one in Maine and the other nearby in Hancock Shaker Village—Habib, an experienced herbalist and a member of the group, has begun to rebuild the herb farm. He says:

> There was no herb garden when we came here two years ago. The Shakers hadn't been here in many years, and those who had lived here after them hadn't been into herbs. I got a few plants from each of the communities and that's how we reestablished the herb garden.
>
> We have most of the culinary herbs: dill, marjoram, oregano, chives, peppermint, spearmint, sage, lemon balm, French tarragon, basil, and others. We use them ourselves and package and sell a little locally on a small scale, but we hope to develop it into an herb business eventually.

Habib works on the herb garden alone and only part-time, which illustrates how easy herbs are to care for. He emphasizes:

They don't take much care, especially the perrenials. If you mulch them well, they don't need a whole lot of looking after.

I like working with the perennials the most; to see them growing larger and older with each season. Perennials can go on for years and years and years, if you care for them properly. After a certain point you may have to divide them to give them more room and to rejuvenate them in a sense. But as long as the proper position (sun or shade), room, and fertility are maintained, they can go on for an indeterminate length of time.

The rejuvenated herb garden also contains a number of medicinal herbs. Habib says that comfrey is a basic medicinal plant included in his list of what the new turning-to-natural-living household should have on hand. Others are goldenseal, ginseng, wormwood, valerian, and chamomile.

"There are a lot of people here who treat themselves, who know a lot about herbs as medicine," Habib says. There's a medical doctor here who knows a little—he prescribes a lot of goldenseal—but there are others who are more experienced and knowledgeable (with herbs). He's learning from them, to some extent."

The Sufi spiritual life encompasses the herb garden. Habib and those who help him out occasionally attune themselves through meditation and concentration with the nature spirits, he says. "We try to work with the configuration of the heavens in aligning and attuning ourselves to what's happening on more refined planes in terms of how and when we work. We just have a very reverential attitude in relation to the plants in the garden."

With this caring and communion, better herbs grow, he says. But not all gardens are tended so. Habib warns:

One of the things that people should be cautious about (when buying herbs) is that, while these herbs are available in natural food stores, most of them are coming from a very few large importers and distributors. They have been around all along, of course; but these people are not growers, and they have very low quality control.

Anything a person him/herself grows, dries, and packages properly will inevitably be of much superior quality than that which could be bought from these large companies. One of the ways things are changing is that more conscientious growers are starting to get their stuff out; the small growers selling to the co-ops, for example.

People really ought to figure out where their stuff is coming from. Once you do get hold of something that has some quality and some substance to it, and you put it next to what you've been buying all along, the latter looks awful. Certain things show in the way a plant looks. It should maintain its vibrant color when its dry. Lots of times the stuff is tan or brown. This is a good way of knowing that it doesn't contain the nutrients and medicinal qualities it's supposed to. This is a result of a lack of quality control and the proper picking, drying, and packing processes.

"We hope to grow to a point where we can employ three people who will be able to earn the best part of their living by growing herbs on two acres of land," he says. "Of course, that's according to our rather altered economic system." Herbs may be big business to some, but to others they are an example of an incorporated and balanced life style.

Each herb embodies "a particular quality or radiance. As we eat them that quality is enhanced in ourselves."

—*The Findhorn Garden**

---

*Reprinted by permission of the Findhorn Foundation, Forres, Moray, Scotland, and Harper and Row, New York.

4

Rooting Around

A friendly forage

It all looks green to begin with—rangy, wild, useful only to block the view of the water. Then the leader gives the whoop of a mountain man and yells, "Hey, come here; look what I found!"

That was my introduction to the Foraging Friends Wild Food Club, a chapter of the National Wild Foods Association, Parkersburg, West Virginia. Its founder and president, Lloyd Rich, had organized a foraging expedition for members and novice nibblers of weeds at Starved Rock State Park near Ottawa, Illinois. The area consists of deep gorges and sandstone cliffs, and is rich with Indian lore. At the edge of the state park are fields and gullies of wild edibles, which the group was out to gather for a feast later that July day.

Among the foragers were twin brothers who produce singing commercials, an industrial salesman, a secretary, a counterculture handyman, a camp counselor, a hotel baker, a writer, and a Vietnam veteran. The weekend began with a presentation by Bob Williams, a science educator at Southern Illinois University and wild food party-giver.

Foraging, the art of shopping in the underbrush for herbs and roots to make a meal, is a matter of awareness, experimenting and a growing inner feeling of confidence that one gains when gathering food from the land.

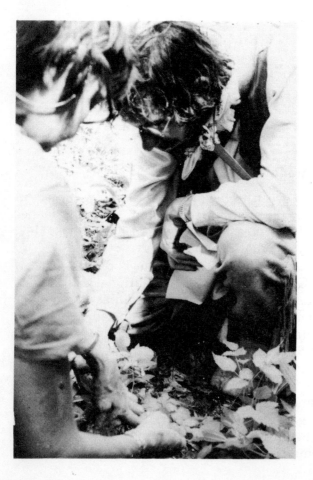

"Finding wild foods is a lot of work," Bob warned the eager but inexperienced crowd of 20. "It's hard to live off the land; the seasons are the problem."

A botanist by training, Bob is not a professional "wild" person. His foraging expeditions range over the vacant lots, railroad rights-of-way, alleys and untended parks of metropolitan areas from Washington, D.C. to Los Angeles. There, in sight of skyscrapers, he finds lamb's quarters, dock, dandelion, mullein, and chicory, to name a few useful herbs. At his periodic wild food parties he has fed up to 150 people from herbs gathered in a downtown area. Of course, there wasn't enough for more than just a taste, but he proved it could be done.

Along with the where-to-look and what-for instruction comes a word of caution about foraging. The standard gathering rules are: collect only fresh materials, carry them in properly ventilated containers, and store them with care to avoid spoiling. For city gatherers there are a few more precautions: be aware that the place where you are foraging may have been used by dogs, cats, and humans as a "water closet." Wash the wild urban foods with special care. If it is an obviously used area, collect only those plants that will be cooked.

Ranging out of the inner city, herbs are to be found growing at the edges of lawns, parks, and around businesses. These may or may not have been sprayed with insecticides or herbicides. If you can find out, ask. If not, a careful washing should be sufficient caution. Long-term chemicals are not so easily washed away. You may check with the park department to find out what sprays may have been used and refrain from picking in those areas.

Also, Bob suggests that urban foragers stay away from factories, which "spew a pall of various pollutants over our cities." These kill, stunt, or damage herbs and plants and make them unfit to eat.

Bob, who does a lot of youth education, acts as intermediary between the young generation, most of whose food comes from the freezer, and those 70 and 80 year olds with the knowledge that comes from long experience. "Most of our senior citizens have time," he says, "and they're glad to tell you what they know. If you take the time to say, 'show me,' they're pleased to."

Foraging is a wonderful skill to give a child, and most kids love it. Bob has taken 80 fifth and sixth graders on greens walks to collect wild edibles. They've nibbled along the way on recommended leaves and eaten up the folk and Indian lore he imparts as part of the lesson. While they walk, he swings a thermos of boiling water into which he has dropped rose petals. At the end of the hike there's tea and lunch made out of what's been found.

"The kids eat everything and ask for more—even leftovers!" Bob says, making his point about the palatability of wild foods as tested by the world's fussiest eaters.

Although he has found a feast around rather than inside McDonald's in the form of dock, yarrow, purslane and other herbs, he has also foraged off the beaten track. And from that experience he has formed an ethic. It amounts to this: take what you like, eat what you take, and "leave a third for the critters and reforestation."

The following are a few urban herbs you might look out for.

Chickweed (Stellaria media), Chick Wittles, Clucken Wort, Skirt Buttons.

This light green plant is an annual that grows near the ground. Hairs are found on one side of the stem only to a joint and then on the opposite side; tiny white star-shaped flowers bloom in the spring. Chickweed contains copper and is a tasty cress deserving of

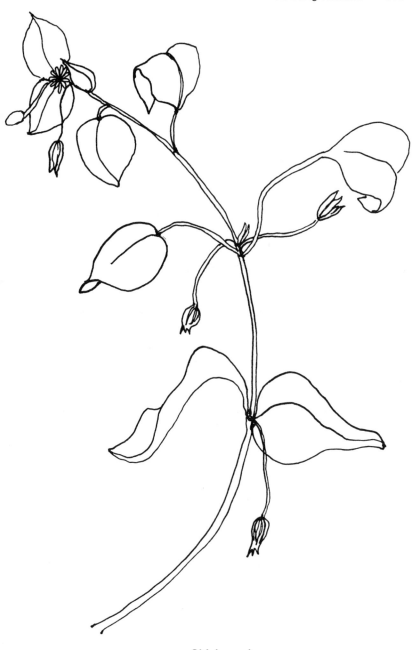

Chickweed

a spunky salad or, like spinach, it may be cooked as a vegetable:

Wash plant
Flick off excess water
Cook quickly with butter, salt, pepper, chives, and a
    dash of nutmeg
Drain and serve with a twist of lemon.

Chickweed tea is known to be a stomach aid, a reducing aid, and an eye lotion.

MARKET VALUE $7 per pound retail.

Wild Carrot (Daucus carota), Queen Anne's Lace

Although this sturdy but fragile-looking weed is said to prefer the seaside, it is found widely in wastelands, roadsides, and fields. Its lacy leaves were a part of the headdresses and bouquets of the ladies of the court of the English Queen Anne. Its white, lacy flower heads are made up of dainty individual flowerets and a tiny central purple flower is said to be a lucky piece on which to make a wish.

Branching from two-foot stalks, Queen Anne's Lace leaves may be eaten in salads, soups, and stews; the seeds may be used much as caraway seed. Cooked, the herb provides vitamin A, good for growing and healthy eyes and skin, and vitamin E. These vitamins are particularly helpful to city folk in withstanding air pollution.

The second-year root of this herb is best. It is six inches long and as fat as a finger. It may be cleaned and boiled, barely covered with water, for 20 minutes. Removing the central core, which is a bit woody, this herb may be served much as its cultivated kin, with salt, pepper, and butter.

Wild carrot

The best plant product is the seed, however, You may thresh them from along the road, putting them in paper bags until you get home. There, rub the seed heads between the palms of your hands to remove the chaff and blow it aside in the wind. The seeds may be used as a flavoring. Powder the seeds and sift them into soups, stews, boiled meats, and goulash.

This herb is also an antiseptic, and a tisane of the first year's foliage is said to relieve bladder disorder, kidney problems, and dropsy. A wild carrot tea following a six-course feast will ease the diner's digestion:

Crush 1 tablespoon each wild carrot and anise seeds;
Pour 1 pint boiling water over seeds;
Serve as a spicy substitute for after-dinner coffee.

Milkweed (Asclepias syriaca)

Like dandelions, milkweed is one of those easily recognizable weeds commonly found in the eastern and central United States. A roadside weed, it grows to about two feet tall and is a sturdy plant with long, broad leaves. In the spring and summer milkweed develops ribbed pods containing the seed and silk down, which will carry the seed on the wind in the fall. This silk has been used for making hats and for stuffing bed pillows. In Russia and France it is used to make textiles. In the U.S., herbalists use milkweed juice to cure warts, swellings, and sores. The powdered rhizome and root make up into an infusion for asthma and typhoid fever.

Elsie Lyons, from Chicago, makes a lovely dish by gently blending the pods in a blender and rolling the resulting vegetable into Swedish pancakes. The results are relished by all.

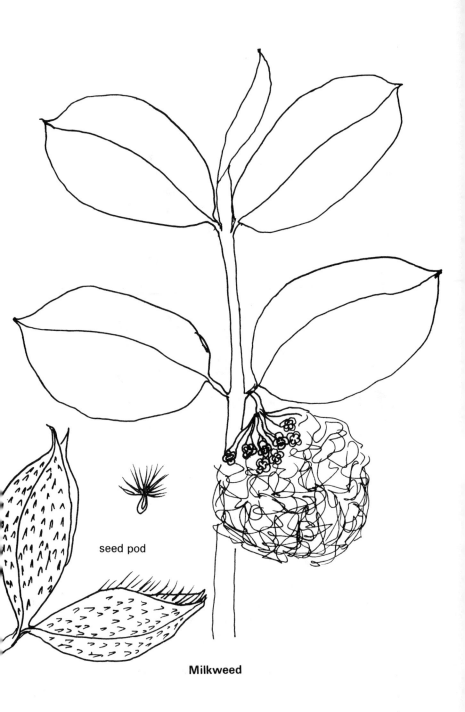

seed pod

Milkweed

Rich Milkweed Crepes a'Lyons

BATTER

Prepare a crepe batter of equal amounts of flour and
milk, a little sugar and salt, and a tablespoon of
butter for each cup of flour;

Fry in the least amount of oil possible or use a crepe
maker;

Refrigerate until the filling is prepared.

PODS
Gather half grown (or smaller) milkweed pods;
Boil in water to cover for 1 minute;
Drain and drop in cold water immediately;
Repeat process 3 times using fresh water each time;
Finally, cook 10 minutes;
Drain and puree in blender.

FILLING
Melt 2 tablespoons of butter over low heat;
Blend in 2 tablespoons of flour;
Add 1 cup milk and preferred seasonings (including a
    clove studded onion).
Cook to thicken;
Remove and discard onion;
Add pureed milkweed pods and slivered almonds.

VOILA!
Fill, prepare crepes, and roll;
Place in baking dish and cover with grated cheddar
    cheese;
Place under broiler to heat and melt cheese.

Wood Sorrel (Oxalis acetosella), Trefoil, Hallelujah (it blooms between Easter and Whitsuntide).

A resident of damp, shady woods, the dainty wood sorrel is also a city plant that is found in vacant lots and at the edges of parks. Its long, slender stalk is red at the base; from it grow creeping rootstalks. Purple-veined white flowers appear cup-shaped in the spring. Its three heart-shaped leaflets (per leaf) are yellow-green on top and purple underneath.

Wood sorrel is a self-sufficient plant. During the day it folds its leaves inward to protect its delicate moisture from evaporation in the light. In the rain it folds its leaves so that the roots have access to every drop, and at night, it again folds its leaves to allow the dew to drop to its roots.

This city herb is easily cultivated by root in a moist, shady garden. Set as a border plant, it will spread freely.

Its sour taste is reminiscent of citrus and hints of its vitamin C content. It is used as a remedy for fever, catarrhs, hemorrhages, and urinary maladies. It also adds a lively flavor to salads. Or it can be a refreshing nibble while you walk through the park. However, the sour taste is actually caused by oxalic acid, which is extremely poisonous in large quantities. Oxalic acid is what makes rhubarb leaves poisonous. Thus, wood sorrel should be eaten sparingly.

Plantain (Plantago major), White Man's Foot

Named for its ability to show up wherever the white man—English or American—set foot, this common weed nowadays favors the cracks in city sidewalks. Its leaves are ribbed and ovate, and a purple-green blossomed spike rises up from the center. Long, straight yellow roots sink into the soil.

A "bicyclist's herb," it is an instant remedy for scrapes and scratches. It also makes a good poultice for insect bites and stings.

Chew leaves until they are pulverized and mixed well
    with saliva;
Apply to scrape, scratch, or sting;
Leave it on a half-minute or so;
Repeat.

Plantain seals the wound and stops the bleeding.

Market Value $2 per pound retail.

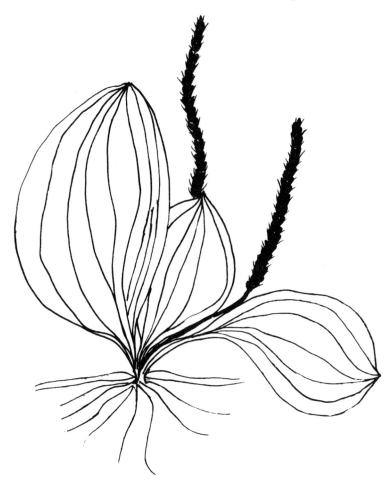

Plantain

Lamb's Quarters (Chenopodium album), Muck-hill Weed, Dung Weed, Pigweed, and All-good.

There are mixed feelings about this once popular herb, resident of pasture lands and other waste places, including those in cities. Once a preferred green—until spinach stole the show—lamb's quarters grows one to three feet tall and has short, alternate branches reaching upward in a spikey form. Leaf shapes vary from triangles to ovals with teeth. Its flowers are pale green and grow on short spikes. The leaves and stems of this plant have a white-gray powder covering, giving a dull silvery effect and making the plant look sprayed or dusty.

Lamb's quarters is easily grown from seed and needs virtually no care. It prefers rich soil and readily sows itself. Although it grows easily in the city and countryside, it would be a good neighbor in any garden, for its long root brings the deep soil nutrients to within reach of other plants, and its wide leaves spread the rain around.

Lamb's quarters contains more iron and protein than raw cabbage or spinach and is higher in vitamin B^1 and B^2 than they are, too. It also is high in vitamins C and A and in calcium. An age-old vegetable for man (evidence has been found of its existence from the late glacial period in Britain), it also has been fed to cattle for nutritious fodder.

The young greens and the tips of older plants are prime for salads. Older leaves may be cooked as you do spinach. The seeds, which resemble buckwheat, may be harvested and ground for flour to be used in breads and cakes.

By virtue of its staying power and its ability to lend variety and food value to our meals, this outcast herb deserves a prompt renewal.

Sea Scrounging

Clams and crabs aren't herbs, even by the broadest definition of the word, so we'll stick to the plant life in and at the edge of the salt water. It is edible, rich, and possibly the food of the future.

Lamb's quarters

Rockweed (Fucus)

This sweet-tasting sea herb is found clinging to the higher rocks along rough coastlines. Use it as a vegetable, steaming it with your favorite seafood. Or try a landlubber's indoor clambake:

Fill a clambake-sized cooker with 6 inches of water;
Boil water and add a layer of rockweed;
Scrub and pierce potatoes and bed them down in the green nest of the pot;
Cover the potatoes with more rockweed.
Steam covered for 30 minutes;
Open the cooker and add clams, crabs, husked sweet corn, and fish fillets (wrapped in clean corn husks);
Fill the pot up to the top with rockweed, put the lid on, and
Steam for 20 minutes.

Serve with generous amounts of melted butter for a meal straight from the coast of Maine.

Sea Lettuce (Ulva lactuca)

Found in tide pools in rocky areas, this large-leafed plant may be chopped fresh for salads (it's tough if left whole) or dried and powdered and used for a salt-like seasoning. Sea lettuce is easily identifiable: Of the bright green seaweeds, it is the largest, and it appears as thin, transparent sheets.

Dulce (Rhodymedia palmata)

Dulce is a dark red plant with fan-shaped leaves resembling a tongue. It is found near the low-water mark on the seashore, attached to rocks, shells, and hitching a ride on other seaweeds. The plant rarely

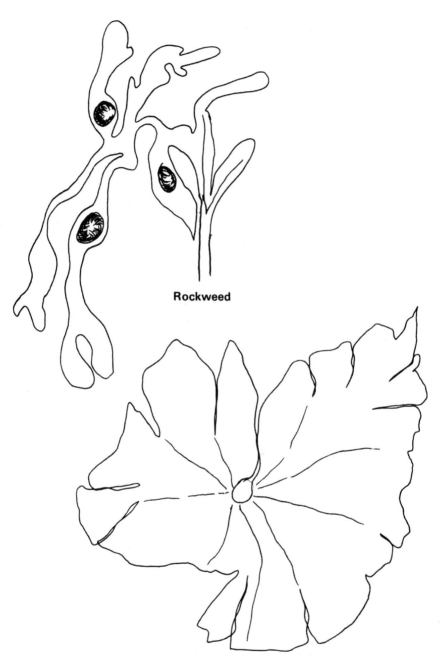

Rockweed

Sea lettuce

Dulce

grows beyond a foot in length. It is rich in ocean minerals.

To prepare, dry to tenderize—it will stay soft in storage—chop, and add it to salads, chowders, and meat or salmon loafs. Or, as the Irish do, you may chew on it as is. It has a tangy taste that will be quite to your liking—by the third try.

MARKET VALUE $6.32 per pound.

Laver (Porphyra)

Another sea-wagging "tongue," this herb is a smooth red, purple, or purple-brown plant with a semiglossy sheen. It grows on rocks, boulders, and pilings near the low-water line on both the East and West Coasts.

This seaweed is grown by the Japanese and imported into this country for sale in Oriental markets and health food stores.

In Japan it is a no-overhead crop. The farmers sink large bundles of bamboo into the underwater sand to give the weed a bed, then go away and come back at harvest time—spring and summer. There is a good market for homegrown laver, and a good living to be made by a seaside gatherer/gardener.

Laver may be used in soups, browned with garlic in oil and ginger root, or stuffed with your favorite ground meat or bean mix.

MARKET VALUE $5.98 per pound retail.

Irish Moss (Chondrus crispus)

This familiar sea herb grows at the rocky mouths of tide pools, and is a dark olive green, purple, or black.

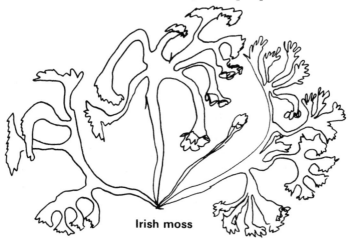

Irish moss

Three to six inches tall, it grows in tight bundles and branches profusely. It is tough when fresh and dried so you must boil it to tenderize. This way it may be offered as a vegetable side dish, or, boiled 30 minutes and cooled, it can be used as a thickener for soups.

Irish moss is used by pharmaceutical companies as a "suspending agent," and it is also known to soften skin. Prepare as a cream or lotion. This is a nutritious seafood with medicinal qualities as well. It is used as an aid in kidney, urinary, and pulmonary ailments. It is also prepared as a decoction:

Steep ½ ounce Irish moss in cold water for 15 minutes;
Add moss to 3 pints milk or water and boil 10 to 15
    minutes;
Strain;
Flavor with licorice, lemon, or cinnamon, and sweeten
    to taste;
Drink freely.

Orach (Atriplex—Several Species)

The lamb's quarters of the sea, this herb looks like its kin, with one- to three-inch-long leaves of a triangular shape. It may be offered up as a salad or boiled lightly for 10 minutes in only a bit of water, buttered, seasoned with salt and pepper, and eaten as a side dish. Orach is rich in iron and contains vitamins, sea salt, minerals, and chlorophyll.

Found among the round stones above the water line, orach is a sprawler in some instances; it also may grow up to 6 feet tall with scaly-looking leaves shaped like giant, dark green arrowheads. (It is a wonder the Japanese have not made a sci-fi film about this one!) Orach grows from Labrador to Virginia and may be gathered from spring to summer.

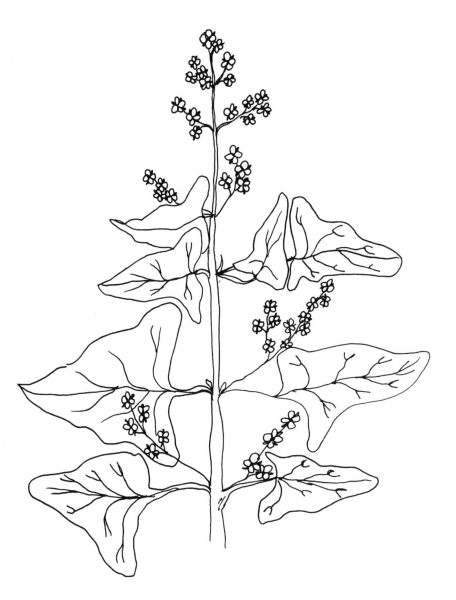

Orach

*Glasswort (Salicornia—several look-alike varieties);
Chicken Claws, Samphire (the English version).*

This plant with the telling name (*wort*, remember, designates medicinal qualities) grows in patches during the spring and summer in clay shore locales and in salt marshes from Massachusetts to Florida and around the Gulf. Only several inches tall, the patches grow together and resemble cactus. It may be used as a salad green. In the fall the bases of the plants begin to turn red but the tips may still be relished.

Glasswort has a clean, juicy taste that works well in a salad doctored with French dressing. It may be used as a garnish with baked fish, fried clams or crab. As a vegetable it is only passable; save it for salad.

Goosetongue (Plantago oliganthos)

A version of plantain, this beach plant grows along the clay shores up and down the East and West Coasts of the U.S. and Canada. It is even found on the rocks of sea bluffs. Grayish-green leaves frame four- to eight-inch spikes of dull green flowers.

Leaves, like snap beans, may be boiled for 20 minutes in very little water and served with butter as a cooked vegetable or cut or broken raw and dressed up with vinegar and oil as a salad.

Beach Plums (Prunus maritima)

A relative on an obscure branch of the domesticated plum and cherry's family tree, beach plums are three- to ten-foot-tall shrubs found in the dune sands of the East and Midwest. In the spring, white blossoms appear and are followed later by red, purple, or yellow-orange fruit one-half inch to one inch in diameter. They may be pickled or made into jams, jellies, and pies.

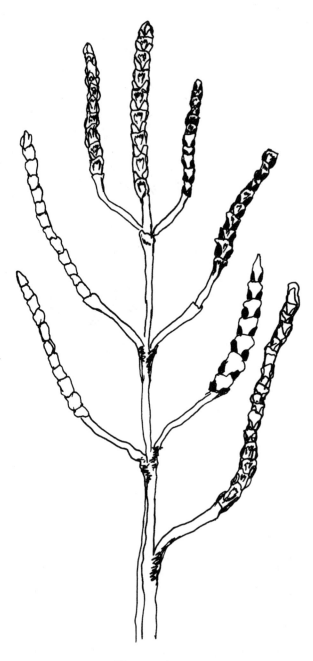

Glasswort

Beach plum

One word of warning for beachcombers: Watch out for what looks like wild parsley or Queen Anne's lace on the hill above the beach. It may not be either, but instead it may be hemlock, and what it does to philosophers, it does to all—poisons!

Seaside salad

Combine chopped orach, goosetongue and glasswort;
Add sour sorrel, also found nearby;
Serve with oil and vinegar.

Land foraging

Lloyd Rich also forages for food, to his mother's despair, in the side yards of Chicago. Dressed in buckskin and armed with a knife, hatchet, soupbowl-sized spoon, and a rock and leather war club, he looks more at home in the woods.

"I'll eat anything," he boasts. "All around is a beautiful world of wild foods. Some are tedious to prepare, but I look at it as an adventure with nature." Raised in Maquoketa, Iowa, Lloyd's unification with the earth began with an issue of the *Old Farmer's Almanac* in which he read that milkweed (his pet herb) was once eaten in high society in England. Now in his twenties and with the enthusiasm of a child, Lloyd teaches wild food foraging at a Chicago YMCA.

"I'm teaching people how to live off the land, to keep them on their feet," Lloyd explains. He describes himself as a realist rather than an alarmist who might be predicting impending worldwide famine. "One of these days you're going to need to eat wild food to survive. You ought to learn how before the last minute," he concludes.

Lloyd takes care to instill a conservationist's conscience and a spiritualist's respect for the world in his pupils. His rules for foraging protect both the world and her ignorant human children.

1. Never pick a rare or protected plant unless absolutely necessary to prevent your own starvation.
2. Accurately identify the plant, making sure you know its Latin name. Different plants share some nicknames in common, and it's easy to become confused.
3. Know what each part of the plant does—root, stem, leaves, flower.
4. Know when each part is edible; pick the part in the appropriate season. A plant's greens may be good in spring and poisonous after the berries appear.

5. Know how to prepare it; some plants need special preparation to make them palatable. (See the bibliography at the end of this book for cookbooks featuring wild foods.)
6. Know the soil in which the herbs grow. Poor soil makes a poor quality herb, in most cases; virgin soil provides a powerhouse of medicine and nutrition.
7. Know how the plant appears in its prime; gather the best you can find.
8. Gather in dry weather.
9. Take what you need and use all you take.

Lloyd's foraging, when he is alone in the woods, must surely be a ceremony. Time escapes him, he says, as his mind turns to Indian ways. He walks into the past toward unity with his heritage, until he is among the mountain men, trappers, and hunters of the past—those who had to know how to survive in the wilderness. He becomes his alter ego, Pierre Du Bois, the French free trader.

Finding a plant he does not know, he looks it up in a battered paperback edition of *Wild Edible Plants of the Eastern United States.* He identifies it and crouches

above it in meditation. He notes its coloration, the placement of its leaves, their size and shape. He speaks to the plant and listens and learns. Backing up, Lloyd observes the plant from all angles, its location and companion plants. He looks around for others of its kind. If he knows a use for it, he will pick it carefully, using his digging stick or a sharp knife. He takes only what he needs and always makes an offering as a sign of unity with the earth. His offering will be something natural, something valuable to him, perhaps a seed that will sprout and grow. (The Indians presented offerings of tobacco when they took a plant from the earth.)

The way Lloyd suggests foraging for plants is evidence of his conservationist outlook. "I take one from here, one from there," he explains, "and when I look back I can't tell where the patch has been picked."

Our foraging weekend at Starved Rock was interspersed with films, slide shows, demonstrations of cooking wild food, and lots of tall tales. Two treks into the "wilderness" resulted in greens for dinner, a case of poison ivy, and a wealth of shared information, from myths to recipes.

Herb foraging can be a solo sport or a family activity. It can be a spiritual experience or a part of a school science project. It can be learned from books, flash cards, or recorded cassettes. It is also an education that can come from characters of the woods, such as Lloyd Rich and other foraging friends.

The following herbs are a few that we found that weekend along a canal and a beaten path.

Cattails (Typha latifolia)

Along the canal, among the other swamp and marsh greens, were the telling brown fingers of cattails, another easily recognizable edible herb. Standing on tall, straight stalks flanked by broad, long grassy

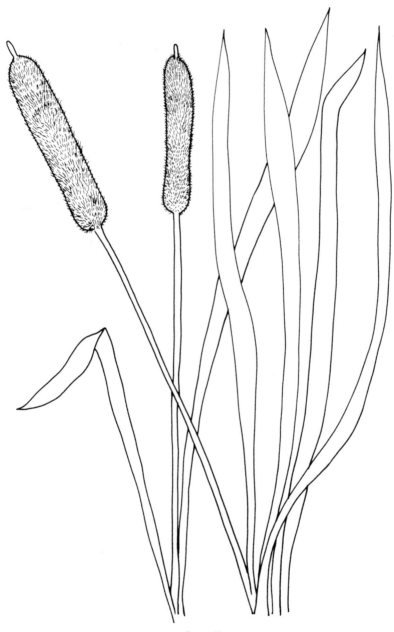

Cattails

leaves, the furry brown flower spikes were ripe and ready for picking.

Actually, cattails are ready for picking almost any time of year because all parts of this plant are edible. The young spring shoots may be substituted for asparagus. Young stems may be added to salad. The bulblike sprouts can be boiled as a vegetable. In August the lower leaf stems may be collected. The roots and stalks may be gathered in the fall, dried, and ground into a flour equal in nutrients to corn or rice.

The pollen heads, which may be used to thicken soup, yield a flour containing protein, sulfur, phosphorus, carbohydrates, sugar, and oil. Fermented, the flour produces ethyl alcohol—antifreeze! And the downy seeds can be used to make pillows or insulate a house.

The market for this fantastic herb is not yet developed. Cattails, can be grown on any well-irrigated farmland. The yield per acre is ten times that of potatoes. An acre of land will yield 140 tons of roots or 32 tons of cattail flour.

MARKET VALUE $3.36 per pound retail for cattail grass seed sold as tea.

Jewelweed (Impatiens capensis), Wild Touch-me-not

This useful plant was prevalent along our path. A tender, tall annual sometimes reaching four feet, it has a light green stem with three-inch egg-shaped leaves. It earns its name by the fact that water beads on the leaves and glistens in the sun. The plant has butter-yellow flowers and spring-loaded seed pods that, when touched, burst open and spew forth seeds all around the area.

Jewelweed may be eaten as an early spring vegetable. The sprouts are gathered when they are four to six inches long and are cooked like green beans and served

Jewelweed

with cream sauce on toast. But the plant's most prominent use is to prevent and treat poison ivy and other
dermatological conditions. Luckily, jewel weed is often
found growing in the same location as poison ivy.

When the skin has been exposed to poison ivy, crush
the leaves of jewelweed in the palm of the hand and
rub the bruised leaves over the affected area. Or, boil
the jewelweed plant in water to form an extract. (This
works even better.) Freeze the resulting juices into
cubes. Apply cooling cubes to the affected area as
needed.

Stinging Nettle (Urtica dioica)

This is another amazing plant with nutritious and
healing powers. Found along roadsides and in vacant
lots, stinging nettle renews its reputation each time a
wayfarer brushes against its venomous spines. The
resulting sting is like that of a bee, and a red rash
develops. (Crushed dock leaves are the antidote.)

Otherwise, this is an appealing plant with finely
toothed heart-shaped leaves on a one- to two-foot stem
covered with hairs. The best way to collect stinging
nettle is to wear gloves. Cut the young spring tops
when the plant is six to eight inches tall; wash them in
running water, put in a pot without adding water, and
cook for 20 minutes. Chop the cooked greens, sieve,
and rewarm with salt, pepper, butter, or gravy. Serve
with poached eggs on toast. The herb is high in vitamins and minerals.

Nettle water clears the complexion and brightens the
eyes. The plant, boiled in vinegar and water and mixed
with eau de cologne, makes a tonic said to stimulate
hair growth. An infusion is helpful in bronchial and
asthmatic ailments and is a weight-reducing aid.

The weed may also be collected for drying in May or
June—before flowering—and dried in a fanned bunch

Stinging nettle

of six to ten plants. When dry, the herb should be packed in an airtight container and may be used in an infusion said to arrest bleeding from the stomach, nose, and lungs.

This amazing herb, once it has lost its sting by drying and wilting, can also be used as fodder. Cows' milk will be richer, horses' coats will have more sheen, laying hens will produce more eggs.

A decoction of nettle yields a green dye; yellow, with alum.

Weight-reducing Nettle Soup

Cook nettles;
Drain juices;
Season juices with salt, pepper, and a little vinegar;
Enjoy and grow thin.

MARKET VALUE $5.98 per pound retail.

Day Lily (Hemerocallis fulva)

Occupants of passing cars never realize that the tall, bright orange flowers are neon signs advertising goodies underground. Day lilies are a good foraging plant both because they are so prevalant and because they are completely edible. They grow in no special soil or temperature and are considered as either tramps or honored guest coast-to-coast.

Two to four inches underground, the white, brown-skinned tubers rest, one to one and one-half inches long and a half-inch around. They may be dug by hand year round by loosening the soil around the plant with hands or trowel. Following the root down to the tuber, break the root off just above the tubers. Harvest the 10 or so tubers and replant the day lily somewhere else so that it may go on growing. (This aids the lilies themselves, which appreciate being thinned out.)

Day lily

Back at camp or in the kitchen, place the sweet day lily tubers in a colander and rinse them with clear water. Scrub as you would carrots or potatoes to remove the soil. Cut off the ends and any small roots remaining. Peel to improve the flavor, wash again, and eat raw for a nut-like flavor, or chill, sliver and add to a green salad. They may be boiled in salt water for 15 to 20 minutes and served as a vegetable.

The flowers may be frittered and coated with sugar. Green buds may be boiled briefly, buttered, and served. Day lilies are especially good in conjunction with Chinese vegetables, served with soy sauce and rice. As a medicine, the roots of the day lily are used as a remedy for ulcers and tumors.

Basic Foraging Equipment

A book on wild foods (see bibliography)
A book on survival
A list of endangered botanicals acquired from your state garden club or department of conservation
A poncho or sheet for protection and for catching nuts and berries from trees
Ziplock and paper bags to keep herbs separated from one another
A notebook and pen or pencil
A canteen
A trowel or a digging stick made from a whittled hardwood branch hardened over a fire
A pocket knife
A pot
A stove
A bowl for fruit and nuts
A harmonica for entertainment
A backpack to carry it

5

Herbs Inside/Out

A Fantasy With Facts

Tansy and Bedstraw Stone lived together in a high-class handmade shack in American farm country. A thick wood cozied up to the back of the house, and a stream rippled and tugged for attention deep in the trees. A tree-round walk led up to a front door with wood latch handle. Calico covered the windows and a cat named the same sat sphinx-like on the wide sill.

Inside, Tansy sat sleeping upright. Straw was propped at an angle next to her, wide awake and looking around at the greenery that was confining them to a two-square foot area in the middle of the room.

"We've got to sell some of these plants," he muttered, and Tansy awoke with the nightmare that she might have to part with her precious companions, her herbs.

Tansy, lucky girl, had been brought up by a hill-country grandma who gave her chamomile tea for a tummyache and the love of herbs for life.

"No, never," she said, wide awake. A lemon balm shivered at the tone of her voice.

"Well, we've got to do something," said Straw.

"Let's move," said Tansy, and so they did.

Not far from the cottage they built a 10 x 12 foot greenhouse with a water heating system and an attached potting shed with some benches high enough for standing and some low enough for sitting, and an old porcelain sink with running water. A wood-round walk connected the cottage to the greenhouse and another formed a triangle connecting a large lath house to the other two.

Straw put up a new outbuilding to contain the new gardening tools for their herb farm: spades and rakes, hoes, an edger, a wheelbarrow, pruning shears, knives, hoses, a trowel, and a small fork. He added flats and sieves, pots and sprinklers.

As soon as the Stones moved the plants into the greenhouse, they started to grow herbs for fun and profit. A natural clearing framed with trees gave them a good growing plot, 50 feet long by 30 feet wide. They tilled, composted, plotted, and planned.

Tansy marked off her herb beds with white lath stakes, and between her 48-inch-wide rows she planted soft grass on which to walk to tend her herbs. (She planted a bit of chamomile here, too, and it flourished under her step.)

"So, what's to be planted?" Straw asked one day as Tansy sat hand-picking couch grass from the middle of her new garden land.

"Chives, parsley, and angelica," she replied. She decided that moment to put in three profitable crops. The specialized herbs would come later.

Angelica (Angelica archangelica)

Tansy liked the name of this eight-foot towering herb whose yellow-green (or white-green) blooms appeared on May 8, the day of Michael the Archangel. Out of the greenhouse came six seedlings. Into the ground three feet apart they went, with room to grow and spread.

Angelica

They did well in the shady area with frequent fertilizing and mulching to keep the smaller weeds down. And Tansy was kept busy all year harvesting angelica leaves and selling them to the local winery to flavor wine and liqueur and to the perfume company in the next town for provocative potions. Even the local restaurants bought Tansy's angelica for their soups and stews. The stems, when candied, went to the local sweet shop. Never to waste a thing, Tansy brewed up an infusion of the roots for Straw's gassy stomach. She also made a stimulating tonic for them both. What she did not sell or use herself that year she dried—leaves, seeds, and roots. And when the plants died after blooming with purple-white flowers in their third year, she began again with fresh seedlings from her greenhouse.

MARKET VALUE $7.50 per pound retail.

Chives (Allium schoenoprasum)

In the spring, in a sunny spot in her garden, Tansy planted chives, a hardy perennial. She planted some as young plants and some as seeds. Later on, she expanded the crop by dividing the full-grown clumps into new six-rooted clusters.

She weeded and watered faithfully, feeding her chives with a little liquid manure after each cutting. Kneeling on the grass and chamomile, Tansy cut the dry chives with a sharp knife and bunched them with no-odor rubber bands in large plastic bags. She placed the bagged chives in a chilled cooler set next to her on the grassy strip.

Back at her work bench, Tansy held bunches of loose chives by their tips and gently shook off the dirt and dry grasses. She weighed the chives into one-pound bunches, tied them in plastic bags, and refrigerated

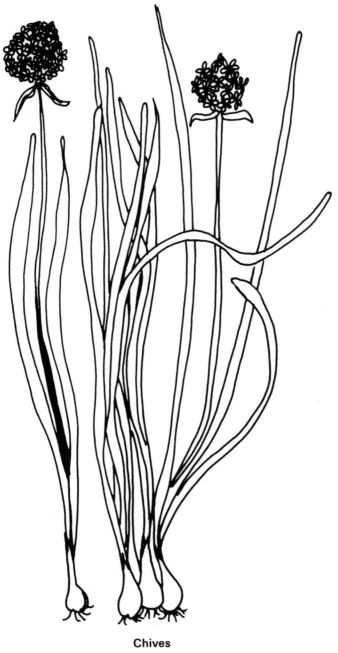

Chives

them. When she had enough to fill her orders in town from family and restaurant cooks, she set out to deliver them.

Throughout the spring and summer of the second year, when her crop was thriving, visitors were drawn to a roadside sign that advertised: "Herbs for Sale." They came in for fresh cuttings from her foot-high plants and bought the cuttings to take them home for salads and dressings, omelettes and potatoes, soups, sausages, and croquettes. A turkey farmer even came to buy chives to mix with his chick feed.

Tansy let some of the chive plants flower with pale purple heads in June and July. These plants she did not harvest; she packed the seeds and sold them by mail all over the country. She also saved some for her next cash crop.

MARKET VALUE $13 per pound retail (dried and cut).

Parsley (Carum petroselinum)

Tansy knew that the Romans wore parsley to prevent drunkenness and that Greek heroes were crowned with it. Through the centuries parsley has been a breath freshener and a symbol of mirth, festivity, honor, and oblivion.

Tansy also knew she could sell pots of the curly-leafed vegetable-herbs to passersby, as well as to the town chefs.

In late February, at work in her potting shed, Tansy planted parsley seeds in small pots and set them in the greenhouse to grow. In April, when the frost was gone for good, she set the plants in the lath house and posted a sale sign on the road. New herb gardeners and good cooks came to buy and set out parsley in their own gardens, and she was sold out by mid-May.

Tansy's cash kitchen crop was started from seed in

Parsley

her greenhouse at the same time as the potted parsley. After soaking the seeds in warm water for 24 hours, she sowed them in pots. When the first leaves appeared, she transferred the little plants to small pots and set them in the greenhouse. Tansy kept track of the root growth, and before they got too tight in the pot, she transplanted them into the prepared plot eight inches apart.

Parsley is pretty as well as flavorful, and Tansy knew her sales depended on the looks of the herb. So just before picking she spent the day nipping off the yellow leaves and discarding them. She also picked off the uncurly leaves and set them up for drying.

She watered and watched for a day or two; then she plucked the parsley stalks off to sell in bunches of 10 to 15 stems to the town cooks, caterers, and local produce buyers. Her price was the same as the local retail price to the cooks; wholesale to the market manager. Her stash was good and fresh, so they came back for more when, in a month, she had another fresh crop of parsley to sell. As the season ended, she dried the remaining parsley for sale to culinary shops and sold the seeds of the two-year-old plants to a wholesale drug manufacturer who extracted apiol for its curative powers.

MARKET VALUE $6 per pound retail

Couch Grass (Agropyron repens), Dog's Grass, Twitch Grass.

Tansy was weeding, yes, but she had plans for the intruders in her garden. Couch grass means "field and wheat and creeping," and surely it does find its way along any ground, through almost any obstacles. It is known to bind the sands of dunes to prevent their blowing away.

Growing in loose ground, couch grass is easy to remove. The root is then cleaned and cut into short pieces. A source of potassium, silica, chlorine, and other minerals, it is eaten by cats and dogs to keep them healthy. And, in human beings, it is thought to

Couch grass

relieve rheumatism, gout, kidney disorders, and bladder congestion. (Make an infusion of 1 ounce to 1¼ pint boiling water and flavor with lemon or honey.)

Couch grass' attributes are curious. A cooled tea made of couch grass and used as a plant food will provide the minerals needed for growth. As an addition to compost it discourages an outbreak of more couch grass among garden plants.

In Italy and France, couch grass is used as cattle and horse feed. We might see the market for it rise in the U.S. as more meat producers subscribe to the growing demand for organically fed livestock. Now, however, it is found only in specialized pharmacies and macrobiotic health food stores.

MARKET VALUE $7.04 per pound retail

From these few crops, Tansy and Bedstraw Stone's business grew. In Chapter 8 we'll meet them again as they set up a shop in town called His and Her'bs. The story of the Stones is a fantasy tale that could come true. You, too, can be an herb grower for profit.

You have a choice. You can start with a pot or a plot, on a sunporch or outside the kitchen door. You can spend a little time or throw all your energy into the endeavor.

First you must decide how much room you have in your apartment or around your house and how much work you want to do. Most herbs take little care, but all plants, like pets, require some attention from their human benefactors to grow well.

Your second decision is based on what grows in your corner of the world. For early success, start with herbs that will thrive in the quality of soil in your garden and the amount of sun or shade of your plot.

Here are herbs that prefer a sunny location: borage, coriander, dill, fennel, basils, lovage, rosemary, rue, thymes, marjoram, oregano, sage, tarragon.

Herbs that prefer the shade are: chervil, parsley, mints, woodruff, lemon balm, costmary, lemon thyme.

Next, get on your knees and dig in the dirt to determine its properties. Is it sandy and dry or moist and rich? Most herbs will thrive in a medium light soil with good drainage. The soil should be able to absorb a reasonable rainfall, and the excess water should run off so that the plants will not sit in puddles.

Prepare the soil with a compost followed by a preliminary crop of alfalfa, fennel, root parsley, or lovage to break up the hard-packed underground soil layers. Then, spade up the weeds. If you recognize them as having herbal qualities, you can make this chore a harvest.

Compost with manure, leaves, and organic kitchen refuse (ration: 5 parts vegetable to 1 part animal). To speed up what might take six months to ripen, add chopped comfrey leaves and turn into the compost. It will be ready in six weeks.

For Homebodies Turned Homesteaders

If you are new to the outdoors, having lived your life surrounded by concrete, you will feel the tug of newly discovered muscles as you work the land. Here's help:

Infuse a handful of chamomile flowers in
4 ounces of olive oil for 1 week;
Use to massage aching muscles.
    or
Steep potentilla in white vinegar and
Use to ease aching muscles and joints.

A Place For Everything

Let the artist in you emerge when you plan the layout of the herb garden. Imagine rows, wedges, wagon-wheels or butterflies. Consider the shape of the lot, the placement of the house, the shade of the trees, and the existence of any fence or wall that might provide protection or support for tall plants.

Traditionally, an herb garden was a place for peace and quiet, a sanctuary for experiencing timelessness. Symmetry is a basic ingredient in planning the garden design. The traditional garden's focal point was often a central sundial. Center your garden on a large rock, tree or shrub, a pool with or without a fountain, or an old wooden bench—a place to sit and muse.

Plant your herbs for visual effect, tall, decorative plants at the back with the shorter, culinary herbs up front for easy access. Plant for colorful impact with yellows, whites, and lavenders together and reds, oranges, and greens en masse. Plant culinary herbs in adjacent plots and group aromatics. Separate your beds with grass or flagstones and border with bricks so that you may wander among them.

If your garden will also contain vegetables, it should be altogether different. Utilitarian rather than restful, this garden's herbs will be of the working class: They can protect companion vegetables. The following chart lists which herbs defend what vegetables against weeds and insects.

TOMATOES basil, beebalm, borage, marigold, mint, parsley
CABBAGE chamomile, dill, hyssop, mint, nasturtium, peppermint, rosemary, sage, southernwood, thyme
LETTUCE dill
CORN lamb's quarters, purslane, pigweed
ONIONS chamomile, sowthistle, summer savory

POTATOES   dead nettle, horseradish, pigweed
CARROTS   chives, rosemary, sage
BEANS   summer savory, rosemary
STRAWBERRIES   borage
ROOT VEGETABLES   foxglove

In addition, some herbs are helpful to all plants as well as to the general health of the soil. They are chives, lavender, lemon balm, sage, parsley, chervil, tarragon, thyme, marjoram, lovage, dill, and yarrow. Fennel is definitely an outsider. Give this herb a place away from others.

The ideal way to start herb plants, especially in the unpredictable weather of the northern U.S., is indoors. No earlier than March—or eight weeks before planting seedlings outside—lay seeds in quarter-inch open rows in a flat filled with clean soil purchased from a nursery or plant store. Do not cover the seeds. Mist them, lay two sheets of newsprint over the top of the flat, and place it in a warm room or sunporch but out of direct sunlight. Finely mist three times a day for a week or ten days. The plants may then be placed in small pots where they will continue to grow for another four weeks in your best lighted window.

If you have purchased your herbs by mail, they will need special attention before settling in to your garden. First, unwrap the herbs and submerge their roots in water; soaking five to ten minutes. Transplant in the garden in late afternoon in prepared light soil. Water thoroughly. Water lightly three or four times until they are settled in the garden. Protect them from a hot sun for the first week to ten days.

Herbs should be transplanted when the ground is moist—just before or right after a good rain. It is also best to plant them on a cloudy day or toward evening to reduce the effect of full sun on the young plant. Pack soil firmly around the roots. When they are set, loosen the surface soil around the plant so it may act as a mulch.

A mulch of cocoa hulls, fresh grass cuttings or straw is also a must for a neat, healthy garden. It keeps the herbs clean in heavy rains, preserves the low growing plants from damage, keeps weeds out, and allows the soil to retain moisture.

Once the garden is started, it will require only a minimum of care. It will need occasional weeding and watering, and you may keep it vital by snipping and nibbling at the herbs. They will respond with renewed growth.

NATURAL GARDENING   Leave plants in their natural habitat; improve the conditions around them to help them grow— remove restraining species from the area and transplant the herbs to spread them throughout the area.

Some Seed Dealers to Get You Started

Comstock, Ferre & Co., 263 Main St., Wethersfield, Conn. 06109
Green Valley Seeds, Felton, Calif. 95018
Le Jardin du Gourmet, Ramsey, N.J. 07446
Nichols Gardens Nursery, 1190 N. Pacific Highway, Albany, Ore. 97321
Send for a catalog and order blanks. Or contact a local nursery.

Herbs as Pets

Not all of us—few, in fact—live in a cottage in the woods with time and land to spare for growing herbs. Some of us live in the city with postage-stamp patios or sunny windows 30 stories up.

Although a southern exposure with five hours of sunlight is ideal for flowering herbs, many will do well indoors with or without the sun. You may supplement the sun with grow-lights—but do not overdo it. Most sun-loving plants should receive no more than 14 to 16 hours.

Select a few pretty pots, pottery or porcelain, in sizes appropriate to your window space and the anticipated size of the chosen herb. If the herb will grow to ten inches, a three- to five-inch pot is the right size (alter ratio accordingly). Pots also may be jars, hanging planters, boxes, or trays. The only requirement is good drainage. If there's no hole in the bottom, make one.

The recommended soil mix for inside herbs is 3 parts loam, 1 part peat moss, and 2 parts sand.

For the herbs that require it, add 1 teaspoon lime to a five-inch pot.

Select your herbs according to personal preference. However, do not plant those that need to freeze to complete their natural cycle, nor perennials that spread unless you want groundcover instead of carpeting.

Your indoor herbarium will need atmospheric regulation if your crop is to thrive. The plants should be kept at an even 50 to 60 degrees (F) with fresh air available but no drafts. Open your windows with the screens at the top, if possible. The humidity range should be from 30 to 50 percent.

Inside, you are the rainmaker, so be sure to provide regular waterings, always watering from the top in the late morning if possible. (If you work, water before, not after.) Spray with an atomizer to dust. Fertilize once a month.

In selecting indoor herbs, do not choose those that are touchy and might die if neglected. Avoid anise, caraway, coriander, and cumin. Select from the following.

Basil

Basil (Ocimum basilicum)

MYTH An herb of conflicting definition—poison and blessing; courtship and disgrace.

MEDICINE Treatment for headache, nausea, and rheumatism.

CULINARY QUALITIES Use on vegetables, in soups, salad dressings, and vinegars, and with egg, tomato, and onion dishes.

INDOOR HERB Bring in the seedlings and pinch back to the first set of leaves. Water well. Fertilize monthly. Pinch off blooms as they appear and use tops regularly. Grows to two feet.

MARKET VALUE $4 per pound retail.

Bay (Laurus nobilis), Laurel

MYTH Provides protection from evil and thunderstorms and is a means to prophecy. A crown for heroes and artists.

MEDICINE Prevents bugs in flour and cereals.

CULINARY QUALITIES Flavors soups, curries, and sauces. Use with shrimp and other shellfish.

INDOOR HERB Place in a shady indoor nook. Water regularly. Repot when roots fill the tub. Keep an eye out for scaly insects appearing on the underside of leaves as brown dots. Wash off with soap suds and a toothbrush. Bays grow slowly to three to six feet indoors.

MARKET VALUE $3 per pound retail.

Bay

Dill

Dill (Anethum graveolens)

MYTH   Used to cast spells and to protect oneself from same.

MEDICINE   To ease swelling and pains, cure ulcers, and increase the flow of mother's milk.

CULINARY QUALITIES   Use flowers to pickle cucumbers; in salads, vinegars, and with shellfish, steaks and chops.

INDOOR HERB   Grow from seed or bring indoors from outside. A feathery green herb, dill grows in full sun in rich soil. Stagger crops so you always have some ready for use. Harvest seeds for pickling and leaves for other uses. Use fresh or dry or freeze to preserve.

MARKET VALUE $9 per pound retail for weed;
$2.50 per pound retail for seed.

Fennel (Foeniculum vulgare)

Myth   Induces strength and courage; is said to increase longevity.

Medicine   For weight reducing. Seeds make a soothing tea for babies.

Culinary Qualities   Use in salads and with fish.

Indoor Herb   Place potted fennel in the sun, watering every so often. Grows 10 to 15 inches tall.

Market Value $2.50 per pound retail.

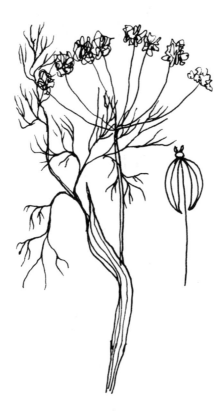

Fennel

Marjoram (*Majorana hortensis*)

MYTH   A symbol of youth and beauty; happiness and grace.

MEDICINE   Extracted oil may be used for sprains; powdered herb makes a sneezing powder.

CULINARY QUALITIES   Tea; green vegetable; with turkey, pork, lamb or eggs.

Wild marjoram

INDOOR HERB   Start from seed; plant with a coat of
   shredded sphagnum moss at its base to prevent
   damping off. A rather reluctant grower to 6 to 8
   inches, marjoram needs sunlight and air space.

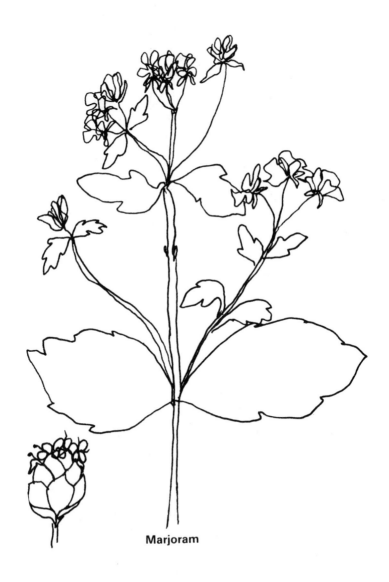

Marjoram

Borage

Oregano (Origanum vulgare)

MYTH Of all the varieties of the genus origanum, no one agrees which is the source of the popular herb.

MEDICINE Relieves upset stomach, loss of appetite, cough; an antidote for narcotic poisoning, juice in the ear relieves pain, noise, and deafness.

CULINARY QUALITIES Besides pizza, spaghetti and other tomato dishes, add to beef and lamb stews,

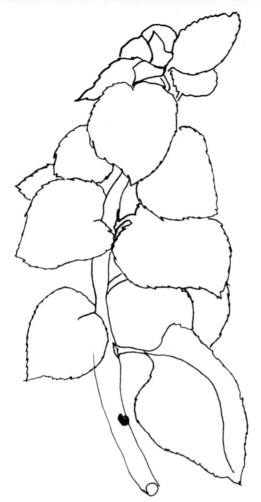

Spanish borage, or oregano

gravies, soups, and salads; use as tea and as salt substitute.

INDOOR HERB A kitchen natural, oregano may be either a white or pink blooming plant. The latter, used for seasoning, is small and tender and resembles marjoram. It reaches six to ten inches in height indoors.

MARKET VALUE $3.50 per pound retail.

Sage

Sage (Salvia officinalis)

MYTH   Said to be a means to salvation of health.

MEDICINE   Once touted as a universal remedy for all bodily ailments, especially those associated with age, now cited as a cure for nervous headaches and sore throats.

CULINARY QUALITIES   Blend a cup of fresh leaves into two cups of a good burgundy wine using an electric blender. Blend until the herb is suspended, and mix with the remaining wine in the bottle—sage vin rouge! Rub fowl and pork with sage before cooking; use finely chopped leaves in cheeses and sausage.

INDOOR HERB   Set in a sunny window. Sage loves fertilizer and limed soil, and will grow to one foot tall.

MARKET VALUE $4.50 per pound retail.

Sorrel (Rumex scutatus)

MYTH   The original shamrock.

MEDICINE   Said to reduce fever and quench thirst. Samuel Culpeper called it a "cordial to the heart."

CULINARY QUALITIES   The French describe this herb by kissing the fingers. Use in soups, broths, and the green sauce below.

GREEN SAUCE

Mash sorrel leaves to a pulp;
Add sugar and vinegar for a sweet and sour sauce.
Serve over fish, fowl, or cold meat.

INDOOR HERB   Plant in deep pots to contain the large roots. Cut back blooms or leaves will toughen. Water daily or twice a day if the plant sits in the sun. Wash leaves with a soapy solution to remove mites. Sorrel is light green and grows quickly from seed to about eight inches with five-inch arrow-like leaves.

Sorrel

Tarragon

Tarragon (Artemisia dracunculus)

MYTH   Called "little dragon," this plant was thought to be an antidote for the bites of rabid dogs, insects, and small mythical reptiles (its roots are twisted serpents).

MEDICINE   An herb used by Hippocrates, it is said to increase physical energy and be a tonic for the heart, lungs, and liver.

CULINARY QUALITIES   Use in vinegar and as a dominating addition to cream sauces, fish and egg dishes, and such vegetables as spinach, peas, and lima beans. A little goes a long way.

INDOOR HERB   Make sure to get the right variety. Russian tarragon grows up strong and stately from seed but has no flavor. Get French tarragon, a hardy plant that grows from a root to about 18 inches. Plant in slightly dry soil in an eight- or ten-inch pot. Place in full sun for best results; spray leaves and water before it's completely dry.

MARKET VALUE $8 per pound retail.

If you bring your plants in from outside, check them at the door. Do not bring in bugs to infest your whole indoor garden. If a few get past you, use the following organic spray to get rid of them:

Mix up a weak solution of yellow naptha soap;
Lay pot on its side;
Spray plant only, top and bottom of leaves; do not spray the soil.

If your kitchen can contain more herbs, please go on. Your meal time will be graced by the presence of old remedies and culinary spirits. Enjoy their presence in the window and on the table.

Sample menu for an herb dinner

Sorrel soup.
Savory omelette—layers of thyme, tarragon, and chives.
Wild onions and potatoes (alternate layers of vegetables and wedges of butter). Season with salt and pepper. Pour milk to the top of the mixture. Bake in a moderate oven—350° (F)—until done.
Lettuce and nasturtium salad seasoned with tarragon, chives, mint, and thyme.
Wild green sandwiches with herb mayonnaise.
Your favorite and complementary tea.
Sugared violets for dessert.

Set the stage for this spiritual feast by sprinkling the water from a cup of steeped vervain around the house just before your party. As myth has it, "your friends will be made merry."

Herb Sweets: the Aromatics

Herb gardening may wend its way into the bath and bedrooms, onto book shelves, and out the door to the patio. Wherever herbs grow they will provide an air of peace and fill the atmosphere with fragrance.

The following herbs lend themselves gracefully to tabletop rock gardens, sand-filled brass trays, hanging pots, or window boxes. Filling a small room, they can create restful and perfumed atmosphere for meditation or quiet reading.

Apple Geranium (Pelargonium Odoratissimum)

Just brushing past this aromatic herb releases a scent and the memories of cider mills and autumn days

Apple geranium

Costmary

in the country. One of many geraniums, the apple variety has small, light green leaves that grow large, round and velvety as the plant matures. It likes the sun and prefers to be watered daily, before 11 A.M., if you please! A bi-weekly fertilizing with a water soluble solution will keep the plant lush and fragrant.

Costmary (*Tanacetum balsamita*)

A Bible marker of the Colonists, this sweet-scented herb rises two to four feet outdoors and is topped with unimpressive yellow flowers. Inside it grows to 18 inches. Costmary likes lots of sun and water.

The broad, long, tapering leaves with fine teeth may be dried and used to freshen linens and be added to a potpourri—or made into a tea. As a medicinal aid, it is known as an astringent and antiseptic.

Jasmine (Jasminum)

The beauty of indoor herb gardening is that you may cultivate a lovely exotic plant under your roof you could not possibly grow outdoors in most of the U.S.

Jasmine comes from Persia and India. A sacred flower of Vishnu, it is an integral part of Hindu religious ceremonies. It is also used in incense.

Jasmine blooms indoors all winter with white funnel-shaped flowers on thin shoots. They combine with honey for cough syrup. Add to water for bathing. Use as tea.

Jasmine

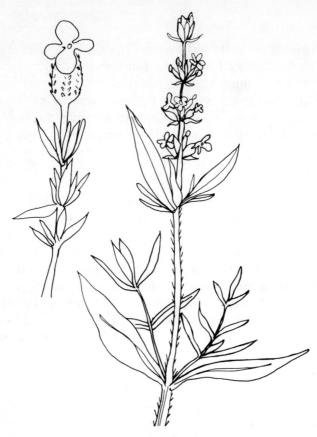

Lavender

Lavender (Lavandula vera)

From India to England and home again as an American houseplant, lavender is an herb that lingers like a memory. It was laid on the floors of Spanish homes to release the scent as it was walked on.

Pot it in a sunlit window, in well-drained sandy soil. It blooms its best in the third year.

Lavender is known as an antiseptic, and its dried flowers were once worn on the head to avert sunstroke. It is also a reviver of the spirit and appetite.

Lavender species include:

FERN-LEAFED LAVENDER   A sunny window resident that grows to two feet indoors and exudes a pungent scent from gray-green leaves.

TOOTHED-LAVENDER   A one- to two-foot-tall indoor plant with gray or green leaves and deep purple flowers.

LAVENDER STOECHAS   Pretty, but not perfumed.

LAVENDER HETEROPHYLLA   Smells of sweet bay and grows to one to two feet indoors. Noted for varied leaves on a single plant and for its ability to fill a room with scent.

Myrtle (Myrtus communis)

This herb is rich in myth and glory. In the Holy Land it was a Hebrew symbol of the highest good. It has also represented peace, joy, love, and passion through the ages. Indoors it graces a room with dark green polished leaves and small white flowers. Amenable to moist conditions, myrtle rests well in sun or shade and may grow to a ripe old age and a height of five feet!

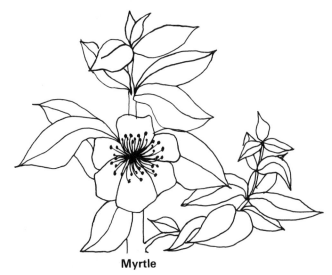

Myrtle

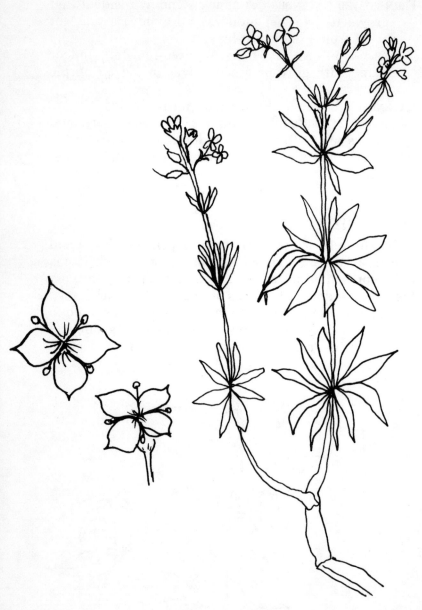

Sweet woodruff

Woodruff (Asperula odorata)

Its flaired leaves—perfect spokes of a wheel—make me feel like traveling to Germany, where this herb adds its fragrance to May wine, champagne, or brandy. A shady-side herb, woodruff blooms with white, star-like blossoms in April or May. To make May wine:

Cut woodruff down to its root;
Add a 3- to 4-inch sprig to
Rhine, Reisling, or dry sauterne;
Age several days; and
Drink the scents of sweet grass, hay, and peach blossoms.

Summary

So, that's the inside and out of herb gathering and growing. How sad if that were the end, that we should sit back idly and watch, mere spectators in the ongoing history of the herbs we've set in motion.

But the best is yet to come: There are rewards to be reaped beyond any cures and culinary sleights of hand. There is a cycle of meditation to be completed. If planting and caring for the herbs flow out of us to these mystical plants, now it is our turn to breathe in and to *experience* our harvest.

6

Picking, Preparing, and Preserving

An herb in the hand is worth two in the ground, and those properly prepared are worth more than pocket change. This is where the fun begins, the reward of the harvest.

But it is work, and it calls for close attention to your garden. You must be constantly aware of each plant's progress in order to harvest each in its prime.

Begin thinking of the harvest as you sow the seeds, repot seedlings, transplant, and thin. Project yourself through the plant to its fruition. In this way you become not just the gardener, but part of the garden itself—feet of soil, stem growing sunward, leaves reaching around you in a cool, green cloak.

The harvest begins early. Done properly, you should be able to get two or three cuttings from a plant in a season. The day before picking, spray-wash the leaves to remove dirt and to reduce handling and danger of damage after picking. Then, early one dry day, after the sun has taken the dew but before it has sapped the moisture and oils from the plant, carefully cut the ripe herbs with pruning shears or a sharp knife. If the plant is an annual, do not cut it too close to the ground— leave at least four inches of stem. If the herb is a perennial or a biennial, halfway should be just right.

Handle herbs gently, being careful not to bruise or tear the leaves. Place them loosely in a shallow box as you harvest and cut only what you can process immediately. Those that you are going to use fresh should not be washed but should be stored in plastic boxes or airtight bags in your refrigerator and washed just before using. Opinion varies as to how long fresh herbs will stay fresh in the refrigerator. Some say three weeks, others project using fresh herbs for Christmas holiday meals if they are cut just before the first frost. You are the best judge. Use your eyes and nose.

Wash the herbs that need further preparation by quickly dunking them in warm water and then a cool rinse. Or, gently spray them to remove the dirt and other grasses that might cling to them. (Short herbs may need several washings.)

Remove the leaves from heavy-stemmed plants to reduce drying time. Dry leaves on a supported screen in a well-ventilated area. (Watch out for drafts that may scatter your harvest.) Shake the screen gently each day, so the herbs will dry evenly. Suggested rack herbs include chervil, lovage, myrrh, parsley, thyme, rosemary, and lemon verbena.

The lighter-stemmed herbs are traditionally tied together (do not mix herbs here) and hung up to air dry. In the attic, kitchen, hallway, furnace room, closet, or shady breezeway—wherever it is dry, warm, and out of the sunlight. If you are lucky enough to have a working fireplace, you may follow tradition and hang

the bunched herbs from racks beside it or suspend
them from the ceiling nearby. The hanging herbs are
sage, savory, mint, oregano, basil, marjoram, horehound, and lemon balm.

To prevent dust collecting during the two weeks or
so it takes to dry the herbs thoroughly, cover them
with brown paper bags. This lengthens the drying time
and is not as pleasant to look at. If you do so, punch
holes in the bag to ventilate.

Oven drying is recommended by some and scorned
by others. The low temperature required—95° to 150°
(F) maximum—is difficult to maintain in some ovens.
Too much heat will damage the essential oils of the
herbs and remove the rich color. If the oven is not hot
enough, drying time will be lengthened, and there is a
chance moisture might collect and form mold. Propo-
nents of oven drying point out that in the two-week
air-dry method, humidity may fluctuate and damage
the herbs. Find your own best way and stick with it.

A fish tank thermometer will help you gauge the
temperature. Its range is 85° to 120° (F).

In the kitchen oven, place the herbs on open paper
bags that you have slit. Leave the door ajar so moisture is released. Drying time will vary according to the
herb and your ability to regulate oven temperature.
Keep an eye on them: If you are drying only the leaves,
it takes less time; be cautious.

Oven inserts and self-contained drying ovens especially made for herbs, vegetables, and fruits are on the
market. They range from $20 to $150 and may contain
room for as much as a half-bushel of drying herbs. Of
those available, the solar dryer seems to be the best,
protecting the herbs from direct sunlight that discol-
ors, dries unevenly, and destroys valuable nutrients. It
also does not use valuable electrical or gas energy.

The solar dryer, as designed by Leandre Poisson, is made from a 55-gallon drum set inside a plywood and plastic covering. The unit can be used year round, indoors or outdoors. Depending on the size of the drum used, up to five drying trays may be installed. The price of the unit runs from $35 to $50. Blueprints and instructions on assembly can be obtained from Leandre Poisson, Solar Survival, Box 118, Harrisburg, N.H. 03450.

If you grow herbs in a big way, why not build a drying shed? It should be large enough to store the quantity of herbs to be dried and should be equipped with one fan with heating element and a second (exhaust) fan to circulate and draw out the hot air. The shed may be equipped with rafters or pipes to hang bunches and with drying racks containing several levels of screens placed four to five inches apart and mounted on wheels for convenience and accessibility. The temperature should not exceed 95° (F).

Two other dryers to consider are stovetop and electric models. The stovetop adds additional space if you are oven-drying and is easily made. The frame is constructed with one-by-fours, and the body of ½-inch insulating board (homasote) is nailed to it. A sheet metal bottom extends beyond the frame by two inches all around the box. Below the bottom is an 18 x 24-inch piece of sheet metal hung horizontally below the bottom shelf using wire and screw eyes. The drying trays fit the dryer in width but are four inches shorter to allow for staggering to facilitate heat flow.

The electric dryer is built as a self-contained unit with five 200-watt light bulbs, a thermostat, a ventilating fan with a six-inch blade, and a low-speed motor.

Mount the above on a ½-inch plywood base with two 1-inch square pieces of wood acting as lengthwise legs. The fan should be aimed to blow across the light bulbs toward the back.

Above this working base, mount a sheet metal disperser and above that the tray—four inches shorter than the box, and spaced four to five inches apart. Do not rest a tray on the metal sheet. The whole is encased in a homasote box with a single hinged door; a vent allows for free circulation. Cover the vent with a ¼- or ½-inch plywood slide to further regulate airflow.

Once dry, the herbs are ready for preparation and storage. Never store herbs in paper or cardboard containers. These materials absorb and rob the herbs of their essential oils. Airtight glass jars and bottles large enough to contain the whole herb are excellent. Once put up, check after a few hours, and then again after a few days. If moisture has collected on the glass, remove the herb and continue to dry it until it is crisp and crumbly. Restore, label the jar, and place the prize in a dark corner of the pantry, cupboard, or closet. If you store the jars near the floor, they will stay cooler: Heat rises. If the presence of moisture escapes you and you lose a little to mold, do not despair. Just discard the herb, sterilize the jars, and store another carefully dried herb inside. If you're successful, there will always be more where the first came from.

The herbs will stay fresh best if left whole or hand-crumbled into large fragments. Powder the herb by grinding fine in a coffee grinder, blender, or with a mortar and pestle just before using. If, however, you are preparing them for sale as powders, you may powder them and store in airtight apothecary jars (with ground glass stoppers). If you are selling through a dealer or supplier, check to find out the preferred level of preparation. Some dealers handle only bulk raw herbs.

Cut and dry last herbs by late September—
perennials halfway, annuals to the ground.

Flower heads are collected when they are fully open. Gather carefully, discard the discolored petals, and spread the blossoms on a screen or framed cheesecloth to dry. Turn occasionally to dry evenly. Store as directed.

Seed heads are gathered as ripening begins or as the heads begin to turn to brown or gray. Check their readiness by gently tapping them. If some seeds drop out, the heads are ready to be picked. In the morning, when the sun has dried the dew, contain the seed heads in a paper bag—then cut the stem four to five inches below the head. Hang these upside down to dry by their stems, heads held in the bag so you do not lose any seeds. The seed heads may also be rack dried on fine chicken wire, old linen, or screening. Turn the heads occasionally and do not crowd them. Remove the seeds and continue drying on a screen if necessary. Store in airtight containers only when completely dry.

Just before using, seeds may be crushed with a rolling pin or a mortar and pestle. If you have many, feed the winter birds and save some for spring planting.

Barks should be gathered in the spring when the sap is rising. Those gathered from two-year-old plants are considered best, and they may be aged for two years more to bring them into their prime.

Roots may be dug in the spring when they are full of life saps, but only if you have no intention of using the rest of the herb. Otherwise, harvest the herb and wait until late fall when the leaves have begun to die to take the root. Dig carefully, using a garden fork and your hands. A root tote may be made from a grain sack: use half for the sack and half to make a long shoulder strap. You may also collect roots in plastic bags so the dirt does not harden and make cleaning more difficult. Clean the roots with a garden hose or bring them in and dunk them in clean water. To dry large roots, cut them into quarter-inch slices or break into one-inch pieces and dry in the oven or the air. Move them about over the three to five weeks they will take in the drying room. Another method of drying thick roots is to quarter them, thread them through the thickest part on small twine, and hang them up like onions to dry. When dry, roots should be brittle and break easily. Store in airtight containers.

Freezing is another way to store herbs. Gather herbs in their prime, wash gently, and shake dry. You may chop the herbs or leave them whole. Place them in one- to one-and-one-half pint-sized plastic bags or freezer boxes. Label and freeze immediately at 0° (F) or below.

Although not necessary, herbs may be blanched for ten seconds followed by a plunge into ice water for a minute and dried between toweling before freezing. This works best for herb "vegetables" such as cattails or young shoots.

When you are ready to use them, mince the herbs

while still frozen and add to the dish being prepared. For real efficiency in preparing a soup or stew herb, freeze herbs in ice cubes. Store the cubes in bags and add a cube of chives, dill, oregano or what-have-you directly to the pot. Other herbs that freeze well are basil, chervil, lemon balm, lovage, sweet marjoram, mints, parsley, rosemary, sage, savories, French tarragon, thyme, and lemon verbena.

To reconstitute dried and powdered herbs, soak the quantity to be used in the liquid required by the recipe—milk, stock, lemon juice, wine, oil, or vinegar. Do this 10 minutes to an hour before using. Or simmer the dried herb in butter, taking care not to burn it and scorch the flavor. Allow 1/3 to 1/2 teaspoon of powdered dry herb to equal the flavor of 1 tablespoon fresh. If you are cooking with dried, flaked herbs, place them in a tea ball or small piece of cheesecloth. The French call a mixed blend of herbs used this way *bouquet garni*. Frozen herbs are equivalent in flavor to fresh, so use the same amount as you would fresh.

Herbs may also be salt-stored in a covered crock with alternating layers of salt and herb, though the advantages of this method are not apparent. Properly stored in a dry, dark, moderately cool place, herbs will last. Seeds will stay good indefinitely. Leaf herbs ought to be replaced after a year's storage and use, however. Jars and frozen packages should always be marked with the herb contained and the date put up.

You can also can your herbs. The following is a list of edible weeds that lend themselves to canning and the complementary culinary herbs with which they appealingly associate:

Barberries—allspice, basil
Burdock—allspice, basil
Skunk Cabbage—wild onion
Cattail shoots—dill

Chickweed—garlic
Dandelion—basil, oregano
Lamb's quarters—basil
Milkweed—dill
Sorrel—garlic, oregano

Drying For Show

Herbs belong outside jars, closets, and freezers too. They are at home in a winter bouquet, pressed between the pages of a book, or leaving town in letters to friends.

Pick herb flowers at their peak and for their color. Whites are found in yarrow and wildflowers such as pearly everlasting and white spurge; yellows in tansy and varieties of goldenrod and yarrow. Thistle flowers are white or lavender; cockscomb are red; bittersweet berries are orange. Other recommended herbs for display are mullein, thyme, bedstraw, rosemary, pennyroyal, costmary, sweet geranium, amaranth, bachelor's buttons, broom, lanceleaf, oregano, peppermint, and St. John's wort.

The seed pods of agrimony, flax, horehound, lily, okra, rose hips, rue, and shepherd's purse may be nestled among the branches in an ornamental display. They should be gathered after the frost and may be dried upright on their stems, loose on a rack, or gently in the oven.

Seed heads that can add much to the dried bouquet are those of curled dock, blue vervain, milkweed, red sumac, boneset, amaranth, chicory, asparagus after they have yellowed, and cattails.

You may air dry the herbs for display. This method works best for short-stemmed, small-blossomed flowers that will not wilt easily. Or you may use a special chemical compound called silica gel. Available from florists and garden shops, the compound may be used

repeatedly for drying large, many-petaled flowers—
roses, zinnias, and carnations for example.

For the silica gel method you will need:

5 pounds of silica gel
A large tray or cookie sheet
A sharp knife
Wire cutters
Florist's wire in 18, 23, 26, and 36 gauges (thick to
    fine)
Florist's tape—green or brown
A toothpick
Masking tape
An art brush
Tweezers
A clear-drying glue
Containers: such as airtight coffee cans, plastic boxes,
    and ice cream cartons; shoe boxes; and cookie tins.

Now, cut the stems one inch below the blooms. Each
will be dried separately. Insert the selected wire (according to stem size) up the stem and into the calyx
(the green "outer envelope" of a flower). Allow one
inch of wire to protrude from the end of the stem. Bend
the wire perpendicularly to the stem and set the flower
with others thus prepared in the selected container.
Set the box on a cookie tray to catch stray gel.

Slowly, with your hand, sift the silica gel over the
blossoms in the box, lifting the petals with the toothpick to work the gel thoroughly into the flower. (If you
do not, you will end up with a flat flower.) Continue
until the flowers are buried. Lift and tap the box to
settle the gel; add more if necessary. Cover the container. Seal it with the masking tape all the way
around and label it with the flower's name and the
date. Store in a dry place.

The gel acts as an absorbent. In three to four days
(average), open the container and gently tip the gel
into another container, lifting the flowers out as they

appear. If some are not completely dry, set them on top of the gel for a few days longer. Make absolutely sure the flowers are thoroughly dry before storing them in an airtight container.

You may have to repair broken petals with glue and reattach any stems that have been dried separately. If they are too brittle, as often happens, use a substitute florist stem, attaching it to the wire at the base of the real one with florist tape.

Arrange in a pretty vase and hold secure with dry floral foam or in a container filled to within three-quarters of an inch of the top with dry sand. Adjust the arrangement; then pour on top of the sand one-fourth to one-half inch of melted paraffin (colored, if you like, with a melted crayon). To preserve a back-drop for your floral display, cut a branch of any length and remove the dead leaves. Strip the lower leaves four to five inches up from the base and cut the woody stem upwards for an inch or so to facilitate absorption of the following mixture.

1 part glycerine to 2 parts water;
Shake very well;
Pour into a glass jar to a depth of 4 to 5 inches
(Mark the level);
Submerge the prepared branch in the mix.

When the liquid drops below the mark, as leaves begin to absorb it, replace in a proportion of 1 part glycerine to 4 parts warm water. When the leaves are oily or drip with the mixture—in three days to three weeks—remove the branches, bunch with others and hang upside down in a dry dark place.

Pressed flowers are as old as love. They are the memory stirrers we come across in old books, birthday cards, and baby albums. They are as out of fashion as parlors and as timely as flowers in the yard.

Select the choicest fine flowers, leaves, and grasses

at various stages of maturity; arrange them to please your eye on facial tissue that has been spread on newsprint paper. Do not overlap. Cover with tissue and again with newsprint. Place between the pages of an old telephone book. Fill the book, separating drying units by three to four pages.

Place the book on a hard, flat surface and weigh it down with bricks. Change the papers carefully daily for three days, then let them alone. The complete process should take several weeks. Store flowers flat and dry in labeled folders until ready to use.

To mount a picture-perfect design—perhaps one with a centered focus of rich hues and larger pieces diminishing in proportion to the outside of the design—select a complementary background and arrange your design on it. Place some flowers "in profile" and others "full-face." Mount them carefully with a toothpick and clear-drying glue. Frame the piece under clean glass, tacking the frame in place. Hang in an indirectly lit place.

By definition, *floragraphy* is the use of the language of flowers. Here are a few meanings to meditate on, to get to know each beyond its appearance, fragrance, and material purpose:

Angelica—Inspiration
Balm—Fun
Basil—Animosity
Borage—Brusqueness
Burdock—Persistence
Chamomile—Fortitude
Clover (pink)—Hurt Pride
Clover (white)—Promise
Dandelion—Absurdity
Marjoram—Maidenly innocence
Sunflower—Showiness
Tansy—Refusal

Sweet clover

To share your love for herbs and flowers with friends, you may make your own notepaper by gluing—in an uncluttered design—a picture of natural, dried weeds to the upper lefthand corner of good quality stationery. Or you may buy plain notepaper and decorate the front flap with your design. With enthusiasm and time you may go on to decorate lampshades, placemats, and even room dividers. The creations will not only let you live amidst your art, but they make lovely gifts of thanks and good wishes. Such products could earn you some income from local boutiques.

Mixing and matching herbs, flowers, pods, and grasses is creating a living collage. Each piece has a story to tell, qualities to impart, history to pass on. Together they express a whole new narrative. It is an old story, and now, it is your story, too.

7

A Mixed Bag

This chapter is a potpourri, a mixed bag of herbal tricks. It is about the side of herbs closest to the heart—the smell of flowers so natural and fine that the best man-made perfume is ordinary by comparison. It is the first taste of good wine after being raised on belly wash. It is a bit of mystery like the flight of bees.

You are about to be introduced to flowers as they are used to cure our ills by subduing our erratic emotions. You will even learn how to keep bugs out of your house and out of your hair.

This chapter is a bit of a test, too. How much have you learned about herbs? If you have learned that herbs are a bit of all of the above—magic, mystery, and dependable kitchen and medicine chest staples— you will have learned the first law of herbs. That is, do not be surprised at anything an herb is or can do. And if you are not surprised, you will always be rewarded.

Other Aromatics

A rose by any other name might be lavender, rose-mary, marjoram, balm, rue, or even mint. These herbs are a few among those known as the *aromatics*. The original use of these herbs may have been discovered out of necessity. In the days of coaches, carriages, and open sewers, fine-frocked folk camouflaged the stench of city streets with a cloved citrus or an herb bouquet held to dainty noses. And, as the bathing practices were somewhat irregular too, herbs were used on the person to mask the musk of human scent.

Today, we may expand the use of aromatics beyond those basics and enjoy them in subtle or singing combination. They can clear the air, scent the linens, and sweeten the breath, but all the while they are also luring memory, stirring the soul, and kindling love. They can be used alone, or mixed in magic potions. Many of the familiar aromatics have been mentioned in other chapters in this book. The herbs that follow are other aromatics. Seek them out and . . . sniff.

Calamus (Acorus calamus), Sweet Flag

Euell Gibbons credits this aquatic plant with turn-ing shy men into satyrs. That is quite a reputation for a cattail look-alike (without the tails) that stands with its roots wet in ditches, and near streams and lakes. Sword-like leaves stand straight up to three feet tall. A flower stem rises from the outer edges of the plant and a flower spike—two to four inches of crowded yellow-green blossoms—emerges about midway down. The flowers only bloom if the plant stands in water.

Sweet flag rushes have been strewn on the floors of churches at festivals and in homes to "please" the air. Medicinally, the herb has been used to treat diseases of the eye, headaches, vertigo, and nerves. It is said to increase the appetite and act as a digestive medicine. As a culinary herb, it may be used as a substitute for

Sweet flag

Deer tongue

cinnamon or nutmeg; it has a spicy and pungent taste.

Found in marshes in the northern U.S., it may also be cultivated in the garden if it is kept constantly moist. The rhizome of the calamus is collected in early spring or late fall of the second or third year. It is dried in a warm room and powdered. It may also be cut into fine pieces to line a drawer or hung in a cheesecloth bag in a closet. It has a sweet scent.

MARKET VALUE $6 per pound retail.

Deertongue (Saxifraga micranthidifolia), Hart's Tongue

This wild plant that smells like vanilla is found along the Pacific Coast in swampy places and on the East Coast, throughout Georgia, and along mountain streams. Its leaves are four to ten inches long with sharp-toothed edges and are edible. They are rather good cooked with bacon bits and served with sour cream. The flower stalk rises two to three feet high and has a pyramid of tiny white flowers. The leaves are gathered with the plant flowers and are dried and used in sachets or other potpourri.

MARKET VALUE $9 per pound retail.

Hyssop (Hyssopus officinalis)

Once supposedly used to clean sacred places, hyssop is known as the holy herb. It grows wild in many states of the U.S. as a bushy evergreen one to two feet high. Its flower whorls contain 6 to 15 blossoms of red, white, or blue and bloom from June to October.

Hyssop grows best in light, dry soil and does well when sprouted from seeds sown in early April. The plant may also be propagated by division or cuttings. But it does its best if sown indoors in 70° (F) dark. The

Hyssop

seeds will germinate in about ten days and may then be moved to a dry, sunny, outside location.

The leaves, taken when the first flowers are about to bloom, are stripped and dried. Medicinally, they make a fine complexion lotion and are said to help heal cuts and soothe sore throats and fever. Hyssop makes a fine tea and may be drunk for rheumatism and pulmonary diseases. It is a pungent aromatic—just as pure pollen must be before the bee transforms it. Hyssop also makes a good honey.

MARKET VALUE $6 per pound retail.

Lemon verbena (Lippia citriodora)

Native to Central and South America, this herb was introduced by the Spanish in the eighteenth century. It is a tender deciduous perennial which, in ideal circumstances, may grow to six feet. Fragrant leaves grow in triplicate like three- to four-inch pale green swords. Pale purple flowers bloom in August. The leaves are gathered when the plant flowers and may be used as a sedative tea, a febrifuge, or a treatment for indigestion.

Lemon verbena requires normal, well-drained soil and likes a sunny fence to lean on. It may be raised from seed or seedlings, but the best way is from cuttings. It makes a lovely facial sauna for all types of skin, and in a potpourri it will retain its pungent scent for years.

Meadowsweet (Filipendula ulmaria), Meadsweet, Lady of the Meadow

A true wildflower, meadowsweet has long been used as a strewing herb to sweeten the step of guests and brides. According to Gerard it "makes the heart merry and joyful and delighteth the senses."

Meadowsweet

This plant, once held sacred by the Druids, grows in damp fields and around streams. Its creamy white, almond-fragrant flowers bloom from June through August on two- to four-foot, erect, purple stems. Serrated leaves are dark green on top and pale and furry underneath.

Meadowsweet is easy to grow indoors and out, but it prefers moist, alkaline soil. It gives forth with pink or dark red flowers in July—the best time to pick this herb.

As a medicinal, meadowsweet has been used to promote kidney action, to heal cuts and abrasions, and to ease stomach cramps. It makes a pleasant tonic and a good diet drink, containing calcium, magnesium, phosphorus, sodium, and vitamin C.

MARKET VALUE $11.52 a pound retail.

Mililot (Melilotus officinalis), Sweet Clover

This wood-scented herb, that frames the smell of new mown hay in the memory, may one day cause a golden "grain" rush. Ten years ago a professor named Hughes discovered a new variety of melilotus in Alabama. Melilotus alba is now under cultivation on more than 5,000 acres and is considered a superior variety of this perennial herb.

Its qualities make it a good herb to be considered by potential farmers who hope to raise a single crop for profit. Mililot resists drought, is adaptable to a wide variety of soils and climates, produces an abundance of seed, fertilizes the soil, grows quickly (blooms in three to four months after sowing), and is rich in excellent quality nectar.

This amazing herb produces the highest quantity of forage per acre of any other forage plant. Its blooms last longer than other honey-producing plants and its

seed enlargement

Mililot

quality equals the best honey now known. According to Maud Grieve, this annual sweet clover may one day head the list of honey plants of the world, if the present rate of spreading continues.

Melilot, the original strain, is a perennial growing two to four feet tall in dry fields and along roadsides and railroad tracks. Small, sweet, yellow or white flowers grow on smooth, erect stems. The fragrance is nearly identical to that of woodruff, and it becomes even stronger when the plant is dried. Supposedly, the same general qualities apply to Melilotus alba.

The whole plant is gathered in May. Besides providing a field for honey bees, the herb can be used as a digestive and emollient. It may be used to treat eye inflammation, and a plaster may be applied for stomach pains. Whole, the flowers may be laid among linens to freshen them or be packed with furs to protect them from moths.

MARKET VALUE   Red clover—$7.99 per pound retail.
                 White clover—$6.95 per pound retail.

Rose (Rosa)

So far, there are 296 species and 16,000 varieties of this "first" aromatic. Roses are the first flowers of poets and lovers. They are the plants equated to the realities of life—beauty and thorns. If you do not know another flower or herb in the world, chances are you know this one.

Basic to any traditional potpourri, rose petals may be collected from any of the many varieties. However, some have other useful qualities. *Rosa damasena* is the source of the best attar (essential oil) of roses, worth almost $200 an ounce. It is possible to draw out these valuable oils at home, but it is a long process and takes 200 pounds of roses to make one ounce.

Rosa rugosa is the source of rose hips, the orange, green, or red pods of varied size that appear on the bushes as the petals fall. Rose hips may be made into tea, an extract, or in a variety of other forms. Drying, however, destroys the vitamin C content, claimed to be 60 times higher than orange juice.

The rose's petals, however, are the prize to the aromatic herbalist. Those wisps of red, pink, or white are the basis of the potpourri found on page 212.

MARKET VALUE Rosehips—
    powder $2.25 per pound retail;
    cut $3.95 per pound retail;
    whole $3.95 per pound retail;
    Rosebuds $8.48 per pound retail.

Wild rose

Southernwood

*Southernwood (Artemisia abrotanum), Old
Man, Lad's Love*

One of the artemisias, sharing space with mugwort
and wormwood, southernwood grows into a three- to
four-foot shrub with gray-green foliage. Though usually smelling of lemon scent, some varieties also smell
of camphor and tangerine.

A hardy herb, this roots easily in any soil in full sun. It may also be propagated by cuttings and should be spaced so that mature plants stand four feet apart. A plant with a sweet smell and a bitter taste, southernwood is a primary ingredient of folk medicine, used to ward off moths, sleepiness, and infection. It also is used as an astringent, an anthelmintic (worm expeller), deobstruent, and a stimulating tonic. Its ashes, mixed with salad oil and applied to the face or bald pate, are said to raise hair. The herb can be used to dye wool yellow.

Spearmint (Menta spicata), Garden Mint, Lamb Mint, Fish Mint

Spearmint came over on the Mayflower. Known as *yerba buena* to those herbalists in the southwest, it spreads by creeping rootstock and sends straight square stems up to two feet tall. Leaves are bright green and wrinkled with toothed edges. Flower blooms are pink or lilac.

Spearmint prefers moist ground, but will grow anywhere. It should be cut several inches above the root when the plant begins to bloom and then dried in bunches. When dry, the leaves are removed, sieved to remove the stalks, and powdered.

Spearmint yields four to five tons per acre commercially, and the oil extracted from its roots is used medicinally. (It takes 350 pounds of spearmint to make one pound of oil).

Although less potent than peppermint, it is a stimulant for the digestive system and is said to allay nausea and ease colic pain. (It is especially used for children's complaints because of its gentle nature.) It is the mint for juleps, and it is used to flavor lamb, fresh peas, and new potatoes.

MARKET VALUE $6.80 per pound retail.

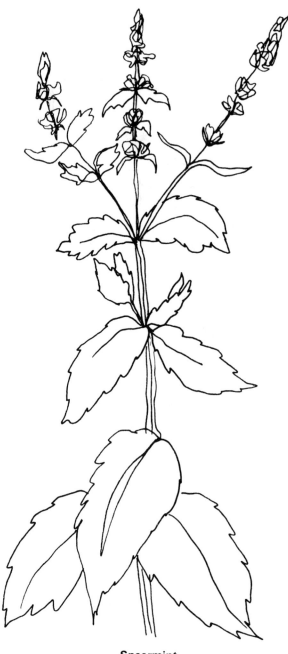

Spearmint

Sweet cicely

Sweet Cicely (Myrrhis odorata)

As pretty as its name, this hardy perennial grows to two feet in partial shade and rich, moist soil. Lacy white flower groupings called *umbrels* unfold in the spring with fern-like foliage. Sweet cicely may be propagated in the spring just as the first leaves of the mother plant emerge. Dig the root, cut a piece of it containing a bud, and replant two feet away.

Both the roots and leaves of this herb offer its sweet scent and anise-like flavor. It may be marketed to the liqueur industry as well as dried, packaged, and sold as a sugar extender. At home, in the kitchen it may be used to reduce the acidity in fruit, or to make a natural candy such as the one below:

Root Sweet

Take roots in fall when the plant is withering and slice thin;

Boil in a little water; boil again in fresh water until roots are tender;

In another pan, make a syrup of 2 cups of sugar and ½ cup water;

Add tender roots to syrup;

Boil until you can see through them;

Drain and dry roots on nonabsorbent paper.

Sachets and potpourris

When making a potpourri or sachet, collect aromatic herbs on a dry morning, cutting four times the volume you will want for the finished project. Cut off the flower petals and discard the discolored ones. Dry in a shaded place on stretched cheesecloth. Dry leaf herbs as described in Chapter 6. When the leaves are crumbly, remove them from the stems. Save the sticks in the cradle of wood next to the fireplace. Add them to your first winter blaze to "flavor" the air.

To dry citrus peel, also a traditional ingredient in sachets or potpourris, thoroughly remove the fruit pulp, including the white, from the outer skin of oranges, lemons, or limes. Tear the rind into pieces as small as possible and dry in a warm place. It is ready to use when brittle.

The key to combining herbs is compatibility; learning it takes time and practice. As you experiment, have patience. The fragrance may not emerge immediately. Like good wine, it may need to age.

Sachets and potpourris are twins separated after the birth of the concoction. A potpourri mixture is added to other ingredients to form a room scenter. A sachet mix is ground into a powder and then poured into pretty little pillows and laid among linens and scarves.

Try any combination of angelica, basil, borage (flowers), lovage, sweet marjoram, lemon verbena, balm, rosemary, sage, and thyme. If you include mint, use only one kind per mixture. And if you add lavender—the original sachet flower—leave out the lemony ones.

Basically, there are three ingredients in an herb sachet: the primary scent, usually an essential oil purchased from a botanical supplier; the secondary scent or blender, made up of dried herbs; and a resin, wood, or root fixative that accounts for no more than one ounce of a two-quart mixture. As you experiment, keep a notebook so when you come up with a winner, you will have it written down. To make sachet:

Blend and grind your selected herbs and spices;
Divide in two;
Add a drop of your favorite essence to one part of the
    mix;
Sniff.

If the mixture is right, add an equal amount to the

other half and combine the two. If the scent is too faint, add another drop to the first. If it is too strong, combine more of the mixture, and it may muffle it enough. If it is still too strong, grind up another batch of herbs and spices and combine with the first mix; add fixative.

Spice Mix to Have on Hand

2 ounces powdered root (orris, angelica, sweet cicely)
1 ounce cloves
½ ounce powdered nutmeg
½ ounce coriander
1 ounce cinnamon
½ ounce powdered citrus peel

After the mix has mellowed over a few days, sew it into plain or patterned squares of silk, calico, or cotton. Label with the herb mix or your own unique card if you are going to sell or give them away. Knead sachets gently once in a while to re-release the fragrances.

Sachets may be secreted in a box of stationery to scent it sweetly, or hidden away anywhere to be remembered when a drawer is opened—a constant surprise.

A potpourri is an elegant extension of sachets. Potpourris are set in ribboned jars to be seen and used when a room needs freshening. To prepare a basic dry potpourri, measure and combine your herbs, flower petals, roots, oils, and spices. When it is right, add a selection of flowers chosen for looks rather than scent. You may select from among dried bachelor's buttons, borage, chamomile, hibiscus, hollyhock, marigolds, pansies, violets, and roses. (Some have scent as well.)

Stir in the fixative and age in a glass jar with a tight

lid in a dark place for several months. Finally, remove to a place where it can be seen and used. Prepared properly it can last 40 years.

A potpourri costs, on an average, 40 cents to make. In a specialty shop attached to a botanical garden, I saw jars containing perhaps five ounces priced at $5.

You may buy antique jars for a puffed-up price or ask at local restaurants for oversized jars that have contained mayonnaise or olives. Or contact a jar manufacturer and purchase a limited number directly from the company.

Save where you can; it is part of the fun.

Potpourri of Herbs

2 cups thyme
1 cup each rosemary and mint
½ cup lavender
¼ cup each tansy and clove
½ ounce orris root to fix

Rose Potpourri

Gather and dry rose petals late in the day, removing them from blooms. Leave the white nubbin on for contrast. Dry on suspended screens in a draft-free warm room, until dry but not crisp and until dark but still the color of the rose. To prepare rose potpourri:

Pound together the following:
    1 ounce each of crushed cloves and stick cinnamon,
    2 ounces ground orris root,
    2 ounces allspice;
Mix herbs with
    3 ounces brown sugar,
    1 ounce gum benzoin,
    Rose petals;

Keep in a covered dish, opening daily to stir;
   After 14 days, take a sample to your druggist and
      ask him to add a few drops of attar of roses to
      your mix;
   Return the sample to the rest of the potpourri and
      stir;
   Set out to scent or refresh a room.

This mixture should last for many years. If the fragrance dims with age, add a teaspoon of salt and a few drops of rose essence.

Perfumes

For centuries men and women have enticed one another with a touch of scented oil behind the ear, in the crook of the elbow, or at the base of the throat. Today, perfumes are a multimillion-dollar industry providing chemically based fragrances.

Natural is best here, too. The fragrance of a real rose or real lily-of-the-valley far surpasses the imitation. And it is simple to make your own perfume, to draw from the flower you have planted, nurtured, picked, and prepared the very essence of its sweet breath. It then not only is the scent you like and others enjoy on you; it *is* you.

To prepare your own perfume, all you need is a glass jar with a tight lid, some absorbent cotton, and some refined (sweet) olive oil, which may be purchased at a local pharmacy.

Line the bottom of the jar with cotton;
Saturate the cotton with the oil;
Fill the jar with your favorite floral or leaf herb(s);
Seal the jar and place in the sun for a day;
Replace the herbs with fresh ones on the second day;
And on the third;
And on the fourth until the oil is saturated with the

fragrance to your liking or until the season for the herb is over;
Store your new perfume in a tightly closed vial and refrigerate to prevent it from turning rancid.

You may experiment with mixing oils. Try a kitchen mix of one teaspoon of basil, sage, and dill oils, one tablespoon sandlewood oil (to fix), and shake the blend with a cup of 75 percent alcohol.

Pomanders

The simplest house perfume is made of a piece of citrus fruit, clove pegs, and spices. Pomanders may be made anytime, but if they are prepared in October or November, they will be ready to give at Christmas as refreshingly welcome gifts.

To prepare, select a ripe, thick-skinned orange (a Seville if you can get), lemon, lime, or even an apple (although apples are less desirable). Completely cover the fruit with studs of cloves—first in a random fashion and later filling in the blanks. Roll it in a mixture of spices and powdered orris root to fix or orris root, gum benzoin, and a little essential oil (musk or civet).

Wrap the orange in tissue and store for one to two months. Or allow the fruit to sit in a spice-filled bowl and dust it daily until it is dry.

At Christmas time, dust it off, tie it with colored ribbon or yarn, and give as a gift. Pomanders may be hung in closets, sick rooms, offices, shops, and even your car.

Flowers That Cure

From scent we move to soul, to the things that disturb it and the flowers that put it right. Having given us color and scent, flowers offer yet another, more subtle gift, a cure for spiritual and mental disharmony.

According to the teachings of the late Edward Bach, a bacteriologist and homeopathic physician who practiced in London between 1910 and 1930, our bodily ills are the results of "lowered vitality" brought about by conflicting moods. Dr. Bach's patients, and those treated with his methods today, are given floral remedies according to their mood and temperament, rather than according to the manifestation of the ill.

Bach developed 38 herbal remedies to treat everything from absent-mindedness to worry. Bach lists 21 aspects of fear to be treated by aspen, rock rose, cherry plum, heather, chicory, and others. There are remedies for impatience, tension, and despair. There is even a "rescue remedy" to be used in cases of accident, shock, or sudden illness.

The Bach remedies* may be used while taking other medical treatment. They have neither side effects nor addictive qualities. The treatment apparently is highly intuitive. It may be administered by another or one may treat one's self.

Bugs, Out!

Tansy at the back step
Catnip on the floor
Clover, cloves and bay leaves
Hung upon the door;

Pennyroyal and birch bark
Sweetflag, thyme and rue
Clean your house
Of cat and mouse
And kick the bugs out, too!

*For more information on this healing process using herbs and flowers you may write to the Secretary, The Dr. Edward Bach Healing Center, Mt. Vernon, Sotwell, Wallingford, Oxon, England.

It makes a lot of sense to use natural bug repellents rather than chemical bug bombs. While ridding the rooms of critters, we are also deodorizing and dispelling stale air in our homes. The herbs that follow promise peace of mind *and* a cleaner house.

General repellant

A fly in the ointment,
A flea in the bed,
A gnat in the pantry,
A tick in the head,
A whistling mosquito,
Your man round the bend
Here's three charms to send them
Outside again.

Feverfew, woodruff, pennyroyal. Try spraying a strong infusion of one of these herbs on the baseboards of infested rooms to drive out the bugs inside, and dose the doorstep to deter others from coming in.

Ants

Red and black ants
Marching off
With a bread crumb
Then a loaf
Telling others of their find
Pretty soon the cook's resigned.

"Industrious, organized, able to carry ten times his weight. . . . " It may look good on a resume for a longshoreman, but if it applies to those tribodied picnic pests, you've got a problem. Three simple herbs will rid your home of ants—catnip, peppermint, and spearmint. Crushed and sprinkled on the ants' regular paths, these mints will head them off at the pass.

Bedbugs

"'Night, 'night
Sleep tight.
Don't let
The bedbugs bite."

 If you can't see them but can feel them, set them up
as follows and leave town for two days. They will be
gone when you get home.

Lay wild thyme on the beds and around the floor of the
        infected room;
Heat the room well;
Close the doors and windows;
Take to a motel for two days.

Beetles and slugs

Beetles and slugs
More creepy bugs
To send along their way.

1 teaspoon eucalyptus oil
3 ounces peppermint oil
3 ounces rosemary oil

 Mix and paint the baseboards with the concoction.
That ought to do it!

Cockroaches

"Scurry, scurry"
"Get the light!"
"Where'd they go to? Where?"

'Roaches in
The dark of night
Lead folks to despair.

These common city pests, the last of which we had nesting in our refrigerator motor, are simple to get rid of. Simply brush oil of peppermint or spearmint on the baseboards. They will take flight so fast you would think they had sprouted wings.

Fleas

They thumbed a ride on Fido
And took a turn with Purr
It won't be long
Until they're gone
And all that's left
Is fur.

If your dog or cat is doing his rear-leg-behind-the-right-ear contortion at the speed of sound, chances are he has fleas. Here is help for both pets. They will sleep better and so will you. Note the different herbs for the same purpose. It can be important.

Dog pillow

Fill a large comfortable pillow with rue, chamomile flowers, winter savory, or pennyroyal.

Cat pillow

Fill a smaller pillow with chamomile and pennyroyal, valerian, or all three.

Flies

God made the fly
So's man
Wouldn't get lazy.

If you are tired of swatting, mix up a batch of clover

leaves, broken bay leaves, eucalyptus, and crushed cloves. Sew it up in a cheesecloth bag and tie it to the screen door. A pot of basil by an open window will help in the same way.

Rats and mice

If your cat at home is lazy
And the Piper's not about,
Try catnip by the baseboards
And send the rodents out.

Mosquitoes and gnats

A humming in the ears,
A cloud around the head
It isn't you who's slipping,
It's ¢)#(—%#* instead.

Mix 1½ teaspoons of pennyroyal oil with ½ teaspoon pure grain alcohol. Do not drink! Rub it on the exposed parts of your body and go forth without fear of these warm-weather pests.

Moths

Light a candle,
Burn the watts,
You're sure to lure
Destructive moths
Who munch on wool
and feast on threads:
It's time to clean
Their clocks *instead!*

Just as moths take to flames, they flutter away from rosemary leaves, southernwood, wormwood, and lavender. Here are several pleasant remedies that will not only keep your woolens whole but also will permeate the air with pleasant scents.

Line a drawer with paper sprinkled with rosemary
    leaves;
Cover with fabric and tack it down tight.
Store therein sweaters and other woolens.

Moth mix

Bag a mix of one cup each rosemary, vetiver (an East
    Indian root), pennyroyal, and five whole bay
    leaves.
Hang it in the closet and leave out the moths.

"Out, out, damn Spot" . . . To repel undesirable pooches, try ginger. You may try a border of it to keep them off the lawn. Cats go pretty much where they want to whether you want them to or not. About the only natural deterrent is rue.

Summary

Herbs are enjoying a renaissance. And they truly are for all men, women, and seasons. As evidenced in this chapter, they are multitalented greeneries that can lure love, calm confusion, and rid us of varmints. These traits, added to herbs' nutritious and curative powers, make them real wonder weeds. We have, at long last, gained respect for those plants we once trod on and plucked up complaining of their interference in our gardens. Now, as new herbalists, they *are* our gardens.

8

Sharing the Wealth

You will remember how Tansy and Bedstraw Stone's herb business grew. Their sign by the side of the road brought in travelers to and from the nearby city, and the same faces began to show up regularly to wander among the neatly patterned garden Tansy set up for show. There the customers could bend down to read the little metal signs next to each pretty herb and crouch to smell the rich odor of fresh growing culinary weeds. Familiarity bred friendship, and soon the rosemary, sage, marjoram, and mint were going home with the visitors. Tansy had room to expand and include summer savory, garlic, and thyme among her profit crops.

Garlic (Allium sativum)

Garlic's staying power is more telling than a friend's

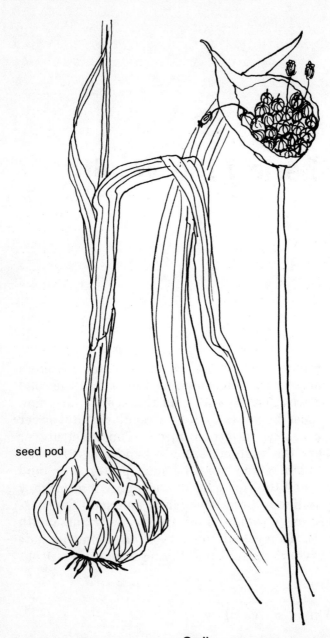

seed pod

Garlic

aversion after you have eaten it in a sandwich. It has been a medicine and a food for 5,000 years, and many legends and stories have risen up around this stinking herb.

The Egyptians worshipped it; the Romans gave it to workers for strength, to soldiers for courage, and to gamecocks to increase their aggression. Islamic legend says that garlic sprang from the foot of Satan; it does have a sulfuric scent.

The garlic plant is one to two feet tall and consists of tall grass-like leaves and a central flower stalk topped by a bunch of tiny white blossoms. The genius-/culprit is underground, a six- to twelve-cloved bulb. Garlic grows best in the warm and sunny climates and moist, sandy soils of California, Texas, and Louisiana.

To propagate the plant, the cloves are separated and planted two inches deep and six inches apart in the early spring. It is estimated that one pound of garlic equals 20 bulbs and that five pounds divided and planted will yield 38 pounds of bulbs.

Garlic is pulled up when the leaves go limp, in August or September. The greens are braided together much like onions and hung to dry.

Medical claims on garlic's behalf should surely more than reprieve its reputation. Having been a protector of persons from the plague in the past, it is now touted as a diuretic, diaphoretic, expectorant, and stimulant. It has been found to lower the blood pressure and correct dizziness, angina, and headaches. Tests in the U.S.S.R. have found it to be viable for destruction of harmful bacteria. Rheumatism may be eased by taking a dose of the following for two to three nights running:

1 to 2 cloves of garlic
Pounded with honey.

Garlic, with its ethnic associations, is enjoyed the

Summer savory

world over in salads, soups, stews, and for flavoring meat. Its vitamins include A, B, and C, in addition to minerals, iron, calcium, and the devil's own sulfur. Luckily, humankind has gotten past its odor barrier.

Odor antidote: parsley and milk.

MARKET VALUE $1.39 per pound retail.

Summer Savory (Satureja hortensis)

Without the fanfare of myth, summer savory comes across as a straightforward hardy annual, 18 inches of symmetrical branches and a lot of good works. Its dark green leaves, shaped like wide needles, may be made into a tea and added to egg, meat, fowl, and salad dishes. It enhances both vinegar and honey. As a medicine, it is said to aid afflictions of the chest such as asthma, to be good for gas, and to ease the pain of bee and wasp stings.

Savory may be sown in April a foot apart in a sunny location in light, rich soil. It should be planted in individual mounds, kept free from weeds while still young, and watered well and often.

Harvesting savory begins when it is six inches tall—about June. The plant should not be allowed to flower. When it does, the whole herb should be taken.

MARKET VALUE $3.50 per pound retail.

Thyme (Thumus vulgaris)

Credited with aiding strength in the Middle Ages and bravery in the French Republic, thyme is another ancient herb. The Romans used it to flavor cheese and to make incense for cleaning the air antiseptically. Thymol was derived from this plant and used on the battlefields during World War I as an antiseptic.

Thyme

Thyme tea is an aromatic stimulant, a diuretic and carminative as well as an antiseptic. A beekeeper's plant, because it attracts them, thyme blends well with honey to make an effective cough medicine:

Make an infusion of thyme;
Cool to room temperature;
Strain;
Add 1 cup pure honey;
Stir to mix;
Refrigerate.
Take one tablespoon up to four times a day for coughs, colds, and sore throats.

To grow thyme, start from seeds in the spring, sprinkling evenly over an indoor flat. Cover lightly, if at all. Germination will take about two weeks. Move the seedlings outdoors, setting them nine inches apart in full sun in dry, sandy soil. Eight to ten inches tall, the plants contain gray-green leaves. Flowers of pink or violet will appear from May to August. Harvest only once before the blooming stage, cutting the plant to within two inches of the ground.

MARKET VALUE $3 per pound retail.

While Tansy handled the customers at their new herb stand set off from the work buildings, Straw worked on the farm, tending and planting the herbs. On alternate weeks they switched jobs and Tansy worked in the potting shed and Bedstraw talked with customers, sharing hints on how they might help their herbs grow and selling them only the best—nothing undersized, oversized, or potbound. He knew their growing reputation depended on it. With each plant he sold he gave away a little cellophane pillow containing another kind of dried herb. Attached to the package was the Stone's business card and a recipe on how to use the sample herb. The next time the customers came by they usually bought a plant of the sample herb. And so business grew, and the community of herb lovers in their locale grew with it.

Several times a week Tansy went to town to deliver fresh herbs to the chefs at the local restaurants. While there, she stopped in different plant stores, nurseries, and health food stores looking for herbs. None of them had what she had, so she sold hers to them. And that is how the Stones got into the wholesale business.

In the morning, during the slack time at the grocery stores, Tansy approached the store owners and supermarket managers with an offer they had no wish to refuse. She would start by selling to them on consignment; then in a few weeks they would buy her products outright. She priced her fresh herbs at a firm 40 percent below retail and gave everyone the same price. Soon, she began spending Saturday mornings at health food stores and supermarkets where she was allowed to set up a table near the produce department. There she gave away samples of herbs in cheese spreads and jellies, and in little sachets. Customers bought the plants and fresh herbs to take home and make their own herb goodies. She agreed to pay the store owner a percentage of the sales profit for being given the space. It was a compatible arrangement.

Soon the season waned, and it was time to dry the herbs. The rafters and racks in the Stones' new drying shed were filled with the rich perfume of drying herbs. Their evenings became a cozy time of making up packets of dried herbs to sell during the winter months. There was much to do. Since an acre of proper land can yield as much as 1,000 pounds of dry herbs, they were literally up to their elbows in winter projects. To get some help, they recruited a local Boy Scout troup and hired a few high school students to lend a hand after classes.

To make time tighter, Straw had taken on the job of teaching an herb class one evening a week in the adult education program at the local high school. Using a slide show format, he instructed interested men and women on the cultivation and use of some of the popular herbs that he and Tansy grew and sold. With the help of the cooking teacher they put up jams; with the use of the industrial arts department, the class made window boxes painted in bright colors and decorated with the Stone's own decal.

As much as the Stones loved herbs—growing them and selling them—there came a time when they needed more help. And just as they needed it, like the cavalry on the ridge of a distant hill, help arrived. Straw was lecturing at a local garden club meeting, and at the herb tea reception afterwards, several people approached him. Violet, a plump woman who only dressed in lavender and white and smelled of English floral perfume, had begun her herbal education when she bought a plant from Tansy. She now had her own garden and was growing and drying herbs for teas. Could she help the Stones and could the Stones help her sell her teas? Clary, her husband, could help too, she offered; he made herb vinegars, wines, and even a bit of beer now and again.

Next, Straw was approached by Fern, a cool, meditative woman with a fresh-out-of-a-relaxed-bath air. Fern made soaps, powders, bath salts, and sachets. Was there a place for her with the Stones?

Then came Myrrh, a pipe-smoking grandfather with years of experience making herb jams, jellies, and candies. Could he and his wife, Ivy, who made candles and incense out of herbs, help, too?

And so Straw came home that night trailed by five eager new herbalists. Together with Tansy, they sat up into the night putting up the Stones' heat-sealed herb "pillows" and stapling them to stand-up display cards for sale in gift shops, boutiques, and health food stores. While their hands were busy, they talked. The outcome was a charter for a cooperative effort, the first step to "His and Her'bs."

During the winter everyone's herb work went on. Violet, who had dried and put up a variety of herbs for tea experimented at the end of the season with blends. She brewed, tested and packaged in five-ounce plastic bags the best blends. Then she went on to test cakes, cookies, and breads that would complement her teas and sell, too. One that she found to her liking follows.

Herb 'n' Olive Bread

2 envelopes yeast
1 cup warm water
3 tablespoons honey
3 tablespoons butter
½ teaspoon sea salt
1 egg
¾ teaspoon dried marjoram, basil, or thyme
½ cup chopped black olives
3-3½ cups unbleached flour
20 whole green stuffed olives

Soften yeast in the water. Add honey, salt, butter, egg, herb, and ripe olives. Blend in 2 cups of the flour. Beat 2 minutes at a medium speed. Gradually stir in the rest of the flour until the dough is stiff.

Cover and allow to rise until double. Toss the dough on a floured surface. Roll it out to a 16 x 16-inch square. Place green olives along one side and roll jellyroll style. Cut into 4 parts. Place crossways side by side in a greased loaf pan and cover with a damp, clean cloth. Let rise again to double. Bake 30 to 35 minutes in a 375° (F) oven. Remove and brush with butter.

Clary made up herb vinegars. He used only the best

red and white wine vinegars, although he sometimes used cider vinegar for a mix that was not so rich. He purchased the vinegar wholesale, and it was an easy task bottling basil, dill, tarragon, mint, lovage, rosemary, and sage vinegars. His job was as simple as the steps that follow.

Blend fresh herb leaves in a blender;
Put them into glass jars;
Pour vinegar over them;
Seal the jars with nonmetal lids;
Label the jars with the type of herb used;
Set them up in a warm place to age for 10 days, stirring daily.

At the end of the aging process, he tasted the vinegar. When it wasn't quite as strong as he liked, he repeated the process. Then the vinegar was strained, filtered, and poured into sterilized bottles containing a sprig of the flavoring herb. Corked and labeled with the new co-op label, the colorful and tasty vinegars were ready for show and sale.

Fern spent the winter in the bathtub testing soaps and salts, and lying in fresh-scented, sacheted sheets. She was the best rested of the new herbalists!

Myrrh went about doing what he had always done but with a renewed vigor, knowing that his goodies would be shared by other people and other people's grandchildren. Among the herbs he used for his jellies were mint, sweet marjoram, summer savory, thyme, sage, and rosemary. He used a recipe passed down to him by his grandmother, who had kept one eye out for the bears in the tall grass of the prairie and the other eye on a bubbling pot.

He mashed the herb leaves and added his liquids and sweetening. Boiling gently for eight minutes or so, he then added pectin and coloring—green for mint and savory, red for marjoram and thyme, orange for sage and rosemary. When the brew was boiled enough, he strained the jelly through cheesecloth into glasses and sealed the jars with melted paraffin. After labeling the glasses with a special sticker displaying the co-op emblem, he stored the glasses on a cupboard shelf and enjoyed the growing rainbow of color.

Myrrh's mint jelly

1 cup water;
1 cup cider vinegar;
2 tablespoons mint;
3½ cups sugar.

Happy as a child again, Myrrh spent the winter making candy sticks for the eager fists of town tykes. Peppermint, horehound and lovage, sesame, and angelica. One herb a week and the rows of glass jars grew.

In his candy pot, he slowly boiled:

1 quart water;
1½ pounds granulated sugar;
1½ pounds brown sugar; and
Enough herb leaves to flavor.

When a drop of the brew made a ball in the bottom of a cup of cold water, it was done. He strained out the herb and, as the syrup cooled, poured it into a buttered pan. When it hardened enough to hold a shape, he cut it into sticks and rolled them to round them off. Some he cut into squares. He wrapped them all individually in plastic and set them away—the new penny candy for His and Her'bs.

In the basement, Ivy worked like a conjurer making candles. Weird and wonderful shapes surrounded her as she worked. They were the milk cartons, plastic bottles, and cutglass containers she saved and scrounged on early morning alley walks and found in flea markets and bargain bins in junk shops. In a corner was a raised sandbox where she played happily making sand candles. And above it all was a rigging of rope and twine—macrame hangings to contain her herb candles. Not far away from her bench were hanging herbs in her favorite aromatics: mint, wintergreen and rosemary and, in bottles on a shelf, imported nutmeg, cinnamon, cloves, and the citrus scents of fresh fruits.

Using a large hot plate, an old pot, and a tin can, Ivy melted pieces of paraffin and beeswax in a makeshift double boiler and added crayons for color—red for cinnamon, brown for cloves, green for mint. As the wax melted she powdered her dried herb with a mortar and pestle and added it to the wax as well. The molds were set in a warming oven, another junk shop find; she cut the wicks an inch longer than the container and weighed each down with a nut in the bottom of the mold. She then carefully poured the sweet-smelling wax into each just-warm mold holding the wick upright in the center. As the wax cooled and hardened she poured a little more into the depression forming in the center. She set them aside to cool and dry.

There were always a few candles ready for unmolding from a previous batch. She tore away the milk carton containers and cut the old bottles from the new candles with a glass cutter. Some of the straight-lined metal and plastic molds she submerged into very hot water in order to melt the outer wax, allowing her to slip the candles out. The round ones she cradled in macrame slings and the squares she set on wood pedestals. Her wares around her, Ivy sat back satisfied and reflected on the homes her handiwork would light and warm.

When she was not making candles or knotting colored twine for hangers, Ivy made incense. This is when she really felt like a sorcerer. It cost her 50¢ to make one ounce and 20 sticks of incense sold for $1.25.

By trial and error she had found some herb scents more likely "to drive the saints from the church," as she said, than to please the meditating mind. Those she found pleasant were bay, juniper leaves, lavender, marjoram, pine needles, rosemary, rose petals, sage, sassafras, tansy, thyme, and woodruff. The spices that she included in her mixtures were allspice, cinnamon, cloves, and nutmeg. There were more, but it was a good start.

Like Merlin, she mixed the powdered herb with potassium nitrate (saltpeter) in no more than 1 part to 10 as the bonding agent. If she used the oil of the herb, the mixture was often ready to form into cones or sticks without the bonding agent. She set them out to dry well before packaging. At other times she found she needed a different bonding agent. She used gum arabic or gum tragacanth, which she found in art supply stores, pharmacies, and mail-order herb companies' catalogs. Adding just enough of this agent to thin the incense mix to a paste, she dipped in long thin splints of wood and stood them upright to dry in a block of clay. Sometimes she used food coloring to dye the sticks; sometimes not.

Sealing these in cellophane she packaged them in long, colorful boxes, her last offering to the success of the new venture.

Instant incense

Buy a charcoal block at a religious supply house;
Set in a tray of sand;
Burn it till it glows;
Sprinkle on your favorite herb.

(Caution: not all herbs will burn and bring blessings to your house. If it stinks, put it out and try another.)

And so the winter passed in furious preparation. A storefront in town was rented and turned into an herb shop. Country scenes were papered on the walls and lath dividers were constructed against which plants would be shown, candles hung, and bottles displayed.

Straw advertised in the local papers to build up interest in the opening of "His and Her'bs" and continued with his club dates and class schedule. Tansy continued to supply the restaurants and grocery stores, and her customers grew. A specialized pharmacy bought a few of her dried herbs for use in special medicinal mixtures, and a barbershop in which customers were shaved amid a jungle of plants began to buy herbs for show and to use in creams and lotions. Tansy learned never to underestimate the potential for a customer.

In the bustle of preparation the herbs were the center of attention. She worked in the greenhouse dividing roots and potting the new plants to ready them for the spring sowing and to sell to customers. And she learned of and began to practice a new trick of the herb trade—bartering.

Tansy and Straw, even with their new partners, could not possibly raise all the herbs they needed. They had neither the time nor the growing conditions. So Tansy began to swap herbs. Through daytime radio talk shows, the local paper, swap magazines, and classified advertisements in gardening and farming magazines, she learned of other herb growers who wanted what she had and had what she wanted. So the mails began to carry seeds and seedlings back and forth across the country. In this way she expanded her wares and made many friends in the process.

Opening day arrived. "His and Her'bs" was filled to

its false rafters with herbs and herb products. A kettle was kept singing to supply water for the sample teas Violet passed out to visitors. Myrrh gave candies to every child who came in and graciously explained to their mothers how he put up his pretty preserves.

Ivy gave a candle-making demonstration that Saturday afternoon and kept the audience spellbound with mystical tales of herbs—some passed down with the plant itself from ages gone by, some made up on the spot.

Fern's soaps and powders and sachets sold well.

"My grandmother used to use this scent," the customers said. "I love the way the linens smell." "I'm going straight home and take a bath in this; I deserve it."

When the cash register was counted, "His and Her'bs" had the sweet smell of success. Customers came and came again. Friends were made. The co-op took on consignments from other herbalists who came their way. They began to show wall hangings and clothes tied and dyed with natural dyes. Dried seed necklaces and mobiles of thistles, nuts, and weed pods hung in the window, and a lotus pod windchime gently announced each new customer. A little girl even brought in what she called a seed sandwich in a jar— burrs and thistles, sunflower seeds, and milkweed down layered in a glass apothecary jar. The Stones put it in a prominent place for display and attached a card with the child's name on it, pleased that the passion for herbs was being passed on.

A beekeeper came in to buy plants and seeds of borage, rosemary, hyssop, sage, thyme, and lemon balm from the co-op garden. He returned the following year with herb honey packaged and sold to Tansy on consignment. And so the cycle continued as seeds became plants, dried herbs, and then pretty and useful products. And the co-op members lived "herbally" ever after. Don't you just love a success story?

Perhaps none of us will ever turn herbs into a thriving and cooperative concern as the Stones did in this fictionalized herb tale, but there are many niches along the way. Perhaps someday herbs will become as popular in the U.S. as they are in France. The French use 10 times the herbs we do and the Italians use five times our consumption.

You might try taking an individual herb and concentrating on doing all you can with it—growing and selling potted plants, dried herbs, and the products you make. Or you might gather or grow several herbs and sell them to a dealer in raw herbs or to a large national or international supplier.

Local dealers are a little like agents. They handle the herbs brought to them by many local people. Some of them do their own growing or digging, too, but mostly, they are the ones with contacts in the big city.

To hook up with a dealer in your area, look for ads in the local paper, "Herbs bought and sold," ask around, or place your own ad. You may want to contact one of the large companies listed elsewhere in this book asking for the name of their area representative.

The next step in the corporate structure of herb enterprise is the supplier, who sells overseas or to retail outlets and individual buyers. Suppliers may buy lots of 1 to 50 pounds or as much as three tons at a time. They may grow some of their own, as does the Indiana Botanical Garden, or buy from dealers all over the country—Oregon, Washington, the Blue Ridge Mountains, the Plains, and the South—"wherever they grow plentifully and wild," says Indiana Botanical's Clara Mehlman.

Like Indiana Botanical Garden, the Magee Root Company of Eolia, Missouri, buys from the diggers (gatherers of wild plants) and the local dealers who act as agents for the diggers. Who digs these days?

"Some folks dig for a living in the poorer sections of the country," says Betty Saunders of Magee. "In other sections they do it for a hobby or sport. You can make a bit of money," she adds. "It all depends on how hard you work at it."

Among other herbs, Magee buys ginseng, goldenseal, may apple, blood root, and snake root from those who roam the woods and countrysides of these United States. The trusted diggers who supply them have been with them for years.

Another supplier who plays middleman is the Wilcox Drug Company, Boone, North Carolina. A father-begun, son-continued herb business that originated in 1900, the Wilcox firm buys 50 to 60 different kinds of raw herbs from collectors and sells to drug manufacturers.

Each year the market demand fluctuates according to what was overproduced the year before—and on what magazine articles have come out with what new claims for a given herb, according to Mrs. Mehlman. As with any other farm crop, weather is a big factor in what is available and for how much.

If you think you might like to become an herb digger, the first rule before contacting one of these companies is to "know your botanicals." You won't get anywhere if you send them a sample of catnip and call it pennyroyal. Once you have properly identified a botanical, estimated its availability, and assessed honestly how much you want to get into this line of work, mount your sample on a card, mark it with the botanical and local folk names, and send it to a supplier (see the end of this book for contact suggestions). Offer your services; let them know how much you can deliver and when. If they need what you have in the quantity you can deliver, you are in business. If not try another supplier.

There are even larger, international companies. One such is Botanicals International in Anaheim, California, the company Wilcox sells to. According to Sam Pfister, general manager for the West Coast firm, they buy their botanicals in crude form and clean them by a combined process of hand and mechanical picking and sifting and a fumigation and sterilization process to bring the product up to U.S. Food and Drug Administration-approved levels governing products for human consumption. Then the herbs are cut and powdered and sold to American and overseas companies for patent and compound medicines.

Today's interest in gathering, growing, and selling botanicals is a natural outgrowth of the "back-to-the-land" movement. Pfister calls it an upsurge of nostalgia. "We went through the fifties and sixties where we took a pill for everything," he says. "People are now looking back to the old ways. Most are gaining in popularity across the board—chamomile, spearmint, peppermint, comfrey, dandelion. . . ."

These dealers and suppliers were unable to name any "most popular" herbs.

According to common sense and advice from those in the know, starting small is your best bet. The herb business can mean big money, but there is competition at the top. You can earn a good living, though—as much as $12,000 on lavender alone according to one source—not to mention the potential of goldenseal and other mighty medicinals. Even if you're in it just for the fun of it and only hope to break even, there's still a lot of room to play.

Besides selling to such outlets as health food stores, supermarkets, specialized pharmacies, gift shops, and boutiques, you may peddle your wares in other ways as an independent. You can sell your products door-to-door. But do not forget to get a license or to advertise. You might distribute flyers in a neighborhood the week before you approach individuals to sell. Also, buy space in the classified ad section of the local paper, put up announcements on community bulletin boards at supermarkets, newstands, drug stores, restaurants—anywhere that people pass.

And remember, education is a part of the herb business. Tell the potential customers how to use your herbs and they are as good as sold.

To sell in volume, try art fairs. The summer outdoor art show takes place on city streets, in suburban shopping malls, at lake sides, or in city parks. They are advertised months in advance by local galleries, in newspapers and magazines, and they are usually planned by art leagues or neighborhood groups. Depending on the age and size of the show, spaces are rented for nominal or meaty fees. You should contact the show's coordinator early to inquire about available space and cost. Perhaps, because you are a "complementary" exhibitor rather than an artist, the fee might be negotiated. If you get a green light to enter the show, try to get a space where your wares will stand out—near the weavers or potters—and where the people will be—near a food concession, for instance.

Give the show some thought. Your booth will be a novelty among the arts and crafts, and with preparation it can catch and hold the attention of the arty browsers. You might construct a booth with hinged sides for easy set-up and concoct rafters for a natural display of hanging herbs. Shelves hung on pegboard at the back may be put up to hold bottles, books—anything colorful and attention getting. Use lots of color to spruce up the greens and grays of the herbs you're selling. Prepare quarter-ounce bags of herbs, plain or mixed, and attach a card to each explaining what it is, a myth or a bit of lore about it, and instructions on how to use the herb in cooking, bathing, or as a tea. You may mention or imply the medicinal qualities, but "relief" is a safer word than "cure."

Offer your inexpensive packets—35¢ to 40¢ apiece—on standup display cards or piled in pretty profusion in a wicker basket. Replenish the supply as packets sell.

Offer prepared potpourris in pretty jars and sachets,

in silk at one price and calico at another. Give yourself a range to interest all who pass by. Have jars available for sniffing and quantities to sell by the ounce. The paraphernalia you will need includes plenty of small plastic bags, paper-coated wire twists, and a small scale to weigh the scented petals. Hand out sample candies and sell them by the pound or fraction of a pound.

Candles, incense, inexpensive catnip toys, naturally dyed scarves, bouquet garni, swags to hang on doors above the welcome mat—these are all possibilities for an art fair herb booth. Just do not try to do too much at once. Get your feet wet and enjoy the sunny afternoon among friends.

Use the fair to make contacts for future sales. Take orders; offer classes. Put out a guestbook for people to sign for additional information. You will build up a following and, more important, a mailing list and a clientele. Have a card made up with your name, address, and telephone number. Decorate it with your own individual herb-related symbol and saying. Hand out a price list of herbs and items you can deliver. Be outgoing. Most artists at these events passively sit back as the public scrutinizes their work. You are not there to be judged, but to sell herbs and to introduce them to passersby. Speak to people before they speak to you. Offer them an herb-sweet. If the unique greenery does not get them, reach out.

Don't stop at art fairs. Try flea markets, garage sales, church bazaars, garden shows, and county and state fairs.

At the farmers' market

What better place to set up summer shop on a sunny Saturday than a farmers' market? This once back street, early morning rough and tumble vegetable show has now come to the affluent suburbs. Herbalists can ride the wave, and as more than a shirttail relative.

"Grown with sunshine and a kiss," the saleslady said, smiling and handing a potted herb to a customer at the farmers' market in Evanston, Illinois. A member of the local unit of the National Herb Society, she and others were there to sell herbs from Illinois and Wisconsin gardens to raise money to send to the National

Herb Garden now under construction at the U.S. National Arboretum in Washington, D.C.

For $5 a day, the herb society unit had rented curb space, enough for two long tables and the open end of a station wagon. From early morning to afternoon they handled a flock of the curious and learned alike. Word of mouth information was shared by those with experience in growing herbs. Fresh plants kept arriving as members delivered mint, woodruff, chives, lemon balm, basil, hyssop, and many other herbs, common and uncommon. According to Anne Koepke: the interest in herbs shown at this market was due to the fact that costs are rising and people are doing more gardening and gourmet cooking.

"Not a day goes by that I don't work with herbs, stripping leaves, making vinegars, potpourris," she said. "That's the fun of it. There's nothing to growing them—you just stick them in the sun and leave them alone."

Mrs. Koepke and five other unit members were kept busy fielding inquiries and solving problems. Questions arose: "What do you have that will go with iced tea?" "Can I grow this in a basement apartment?" "Here's a list of what I have. What else do I need?" The last question came from a young father of two, a new and eager herbalist with a growing garden and a growing family.

"There is nothing like knowing other herb people," one visitor said. "They are the greatest people in the world, more than willing to share their knowledge." And know-how was certainly exchanged that day— enough to fill a recipe file, a garden book, and a pamphlet on human relations.

Most of the potted plants were being sold for less than a dollar. Dried bunches of yarrow and wheat tied up with a few small cattails in a plaid ribbon went for the top price. Other bouquets were made up of grasses, seeded goldenrod, and sumac in red velvet ribbons. Sachets sold for $1.25. The information was free.

In all, the herb society unit took in $450 for one day's work at the farmers' market; perhaps enough to dedicate a brick path at the national garden.

Herbs are a business for Bonnie and Dave Fisher of Peterstown, West Virginia. Most of their land is devoted to fruit, chickens, cows, and geese, but herbs make up what might be considered a good sized garden. On far less than an acre of land, they grow more than 100 different varieties of herbs, mostly the culinary and aromatic types.

From these herbs Bonnie makes teas, salad dressings, vinegars, potpourris, sachets, and many other products. She also sells potted herb plants and seeds directly and by mail.

"Our teas are the most popular," she says. "I'm not too much into medicinal herbs; it's such a complicated field."

Twice a year the Fishers attend an arts and crafts show in their state. For from $25 to $50 they rent space for a booth for four to five days. Their products range in price from 50¢ to $1.50, based on market rates. After subtracting a 15 percent commission for the sponsors, their sales at the fair pay them back their registration fee, and more.

But for the Fishers, there is more than money in growing herbs. "The appeal is just growing the different plants; and doing different things with them. I like to experiment," Bonnie says. They have no plans to expand their already healthy concern. "We want to keep it small. We could go to one show a week, but we just can't get away from the farm that often."

The herb business is thriving and beginning to get crowded. Trained as a teacher and chemist, respectively, Bonnie and Dave started five years ago when "it was a good time. Now it seems that at every art and

craft fair, there are more and more herbs being sold. The market can only take so much."

She advises new herb marketers to "be careful. It's something you've got to try for yourself. If you make it, you make it; if you don't you don't," she says. It's a bit of old homespun philosophy as good now as then.*

---

*For information about herbs and how to grow and use them you may write Hickory Hollow, Rt. 1, Box 52, Peterstown, W. Va. 24963. Send 25¢ for a brochure and/or $2.50 for Bonnie's book, *Herbs Are for Everyone.*

Mail-order herbs

For those folks who would rather talk to plants than people, there is mail-order herb selling. This type of selling is best promoted through magazines that feature gardening and food articles and recipes. Other publications include health magazines and your state farm newspaper. You may key your ads by adding a letter to the number of your street address or referring to a different department number through each ad. This way you will know which ads are drawing and which are not.

It may take several appearances of an ad before you get results; after it has drawn for a while, responses will probably taper off. You may then either change your ad copy or switch publications.

Write a lively ad, hooking the people's interest but avoiding overused, puffed-up phrases. Keep to the facts, but add verve.

The best means to mail plants is by parcel post with special handling, air parcel post, or ship by bus, air freight, or United Parcel Service. Check with local authorities for regulations governing the sale of plants across state lines. All plants sold—especially those sent by mail—should be of your best stock. Make sure the root system is good and strong. You may wrap the roots in dampened sphagnum moss and tie the moss to secure it. Then tie the whole root system into a plastic bag to protect it further. If you are sending many herbs to one customer, pack them in partitioned liquor and wine boxes. Ventilate the box by punching some holes in the sides and be sure to mark the top of the box clearly so your plants arrive the way you packed them, upright and undamaged.

Mail-order marketing is best done in the warm weather months, those falling between the last frost before spring and the first frost before winter. Otherwise, you run the risk of frostbite if the plants are left on a cold loading dock somewhere between you and your customer.

According to the author of a pamphlet on growing herbs for profit, the way to price your herbs for mail order is to charge four times the plants' original cost. This takes into account packaging, postage, stock price, and advertising.

Keep a mailing list of your customers, even those who just send a query. (Drop them from your catalog mailings, however, if they do not buy after a couple of announcements have gone out.) Send out a periodic catalog—neat and short—outlining new prices and new products.

Profit is only one motive for getting into the herb business. Granted, it is a reward, but others lie in less tangible areas of pleasure. An involvement with the growth process, a connection with an ancient art form, a knowledge that by producing quality herbs you are promoting the health, welfare, enjoyment, and education of others whom you may never meet are three good reasons for investing your time in this business.

Sow and sell. It is a grand old game and herbs are their own reward.

9

Hunters, Gatherers, and Herbalists

This is no time to be alone. Now that you've found your way into the world of herbs, there are others with whom you may share your enthusiasm and knowledge and from whom you may learn still more.

You might take a night course in herbology or botany at a high school or university. Ask the folks in the health food store about who supplies their herbs. If it's a local person ask for his or her name and give the person a call. You might ask to see their garden. Who knows, you might even get a few cuttings.

Call an arboretum and ask about herb classes. They may be able to give you the name of a teacher and invite you to see their herb garden display. Look in on their library while you're there. Call up a local learning exchange, a non-profit group that matches people with similar interests.

Contact—or get a job at—a vegetarian restaurant.

Find out what they might be willing to buy and grow it. Collect vegetarian recipes to go along with the herbs you grow. Offer classes through a local health food store; you'll be surprised at how much you know and how much you learn by teaching others.

Don't write off large department stores with gourmet cookware sections. Offer to give a demonstration during lunch hour. Perform with your wares. You can sell herbs and plants (as well as the department's cookware and cookbooks). Work up a banter about the herbs you are using—myth, lore, and medicine. With luck you'll be asked back.

Find out who's giving cooking classes and where. Check the fish market, department stores, night schools. Invite yourself in as a specialist to talk about herbs. Take palatable samples with you. And offer plants and herb products for sale after your demonstration.

Become a member of the Herb Society of America, 300 Massachusetts Ave., Boston, Mass. 02115. According to past executive secretary Lorraine B. Clark most of the members of the society are amateur gardeners, so you should feel right at home. You might write to the society asking for the name of the person in your area who heads the local unit. If there is none, you might organize one.

Another way to get in contact with a group might be through your town seed and bulb store; they should know of an herb organization in the area. And while you're there, don't be afraid to ask questions.

If you are adventurous, contact a coven. Witches have long been known for their familiarity with herbs. For ages they have been misunderstood healers made strange by rejection. You may find among them a guru on the path to herbs.

If wild food hunting interests you, contact the National Wild Foods Association, Edline Wood, 3404 Hemlock Ave., Parkersburg, W.Va. 26101.

Lloyd Rich of Foraging Friends, mentioned in Chapter 4, may also provide names of wild food gatherers across the country. Both groups have an annual outdoor seminar. Contact the Foraging Friends Club, Lloyd Rich, 5648 N. Winthrop, Chicago, Ill. 60660.

In several schools on this continent, serious herbalists are preparing to improve the human condition by learning to cure their own and other's ills. One such school is Green Vale Herbal College in British Columbia. Organized in 1976 by Norma Myers, a teacher of herbology for 10 years, the school is one among a very few of its kind in North America whose purpose it is to prepare people to be herbalists.

"Some people just take the correspondence course to get enough knowledge for their own use—to help their families," Ms. Meyers says. "Others seek to help their friends and communities. And some people definitely intend to become practicing herbalists. If they can do the first course, then we let them take the next step, a one-month clinical experience," she adds. "They take another 15 lessons of practical work in dealing with a patient. Then for two weeks they attend the clinic as an assistant. The course includes things that couldn't be learned in correspondence work."

Because the school is still small, with only three attending teachers, there is room for only 10 students at a time in the one-month practical experience.

After the clinical work is completed, each student receives a personal interview at which time he or she is given a probationary report on his or her accomplishments. An affirmative report recommends the student for an apprenticeship with a practicing herbalist.

Unfortunately, this is the first stumbling block. Because there are few states that allow herbalists the right to practice, finding an apprenticeship is a major frustration. Things are changing, however.

"Right now, because of the heavy pressure, there are going to be lots of states that have new laws (allowing herbalists to practice)," Ms. Myers says. "With herbal-ism opening up, people will have a wider choice about the type of medical care they can get."

Norma Myers is working to make a place in orga-nized medicine for herbalists. She says she will model her efforts after those of chiropractors. "For 14 years we have watched their methods, and now I know the way to get herbalists' acts passed, too. You can't stop democracy," Ms. Myers adds. "If democratic people have a foothold at all, they'll get what they want eventually. Right now the climate is very much in favor of freedom of choice for the consumer. The dem-ocratic right of the people is to have any healer of their choice."

In British Columbia there are herb societies, and boards of practitioners that include registrars and examiners who control the practice of herbalism. "Her-balism will be in the hands of herbalists, not under doctors," Ms. Myers asserts.

Assuming the barriers fall and a student herbalist finds a practitioner with whom to apprentice for a year, what next? Just like all medical practitioners, they hang out a shingle.

"Once you are trained, by apprenticeship or other-wise, you simply open up your office and hang out your sign. The first thing is getting your first patient," Ms. Myers says. "Once you have the first, that person will refer other people to you."

The length of the course of study through the Green Vale Herbal College is variable. "The good ones can do it in 30 days," she says. "Others might take a year. The advanced course is getting out there and healing; just doing it. The spiritual aspect is extremely important to me," she says, "because you can't have a good spirit in a weak body. We have to build a new society. Once people are healed and rebalanced and cleaned up, we'll have beautiful and well-balanced people."

For more information about the study course and annual seminar, write Green Vale Herbal College, Box 319, Alert Bay, B.C., Canada.

Another source of education in herbs is the College of Health Sciences at Bernadean University. Joseph M. Kadans, director of the college, oversees the course of study leading to the Doctor of Naturopathy degree. Herbs are a part of the course of study that also includes nutrition and a general knowledge of chemistry, neurology, pathology and related subjects—enough to better understand the herbology part of the course. Open to high school graduates, the course of study does not have a regimented time frame.

"It's up to the student, his or her ability and background (as to how long the course takes)," Kadans says. "If the student wants to spend a lot of time on it, the course can be completed rather quickly. It depends on just how fast one can assimilate this material. We don't require that a person spend so many years, so many hours in a classroom. The thinking is to take each student individually and to give him or her as much education as can be absorbed."

Naturopaths treat disease by natural medication and nutrition and other nonsurgical means. Naturopathy is a readjustment of the body and a treatment of the whole person using nature's forces—light, water, vibration, heat, electricity, massage, air, and diet.

"Our natural therapy course also includes such subjects as Swedish massage and some exercises," Kadans says. "We do give instruction in problem solving, but we advocate the general wholistic approach, including recreation and a spiritual attitude."

Like herbalists, naturopaths are struggling to surface as an alternative to standard medical care. The subject of licensing is a touchy one. State laws vary. Nevada, where Kadans has his central office, recognizes herbalism and naturopathy as alternate treatment methods. You may find out how your own and other states stand by visiting the county courthouse library. In the states' statutes books, look in the index under herbalism.

Through Kadans' school, students are encouraged to take both naturopathy and theology courses to gain a degree as a medical missionary. With these credentials, he claims, "they can operate (meaning, conduct their healing practice) in any state without any interference."

The Nevada school is one of about 40 independent schools affiliated with Bernadean University. For the name of a school near you and for further information about the study of naturopathy write Bernadean University, 13615 Victory Boulevard, Suites 1113 and 1114, Van Nuys, Calif. 91401.

A living embodiment of the adage, "physician, heal thyself," is John Raymond Christopher, whose suffering from rheumatoid arthritis from birth led him to become a proponent of natural healing. When, after 35 years of debilitating pain, he was given only a few more years to live, he says he sought God's help by helping himself—to an education.

He received a master herbalist degree from Dominion Herbal College in Vancouver, British Columbia, and as he practiced, he preached. As his health improved, he devoted it to the science that had cured him—herbalism. He went on to study at the Institute of Drugless Therapy, received a degree in naturopathy and, in 1950, graduated from the Los Angeles Herbal Institute as an herbal pharmacist.

He opened his own school and has compiled a book for students and practitioners of herbalism. It is *School of Natural Healing: The Reference Volume on Natural Herbs for the Teacher, Student or Herbal Practitioner* (published by Biworld, 1976). Order for $39.95 from Christopher, P.O. Box 352, Provo, Utah 84601.

For information on legislation affecting herb distri-
bution and herbal practices, write National Health
Federation, P.O. Box 688, Monrovia, Calif. 91016.

Some other sources of herbal education follow. You
are advised to contact a local center for a listing of
those in your immediate area.

Boston Center of the Healing Arts
1 Park Place
Boston, Mass. 02109
(Includes herb study)

Church of the Tree of Life
451 Columbus Avenue
San Francisco, Calif. 94101
(Herb studies)

Ms. Ella Birzneck
Dominion Herbal College
7527 Kingsway
Burnaby, B. C.
V3N 3C1
Canada

East/West Foundation
440 Boylston Street
Brookline, Mass. 02146
(Includes classes in herbology)

Herbalist Institute
Box 968
Glendora, Calif. 91740

Manna Natural Foods
4549 E. Hastings
Burnaby, B.C.
V5C 2K3
(Herb classes; Bach remedies study)

National College of Naturopathic Medicine
College of Emporia
Emporia, Kansas 66801

National Institute of Medical Herbalists
19 Cavendish Gardens
Barking, Essex, England
(Founded in 1864, this school/society consists of individual members who treat one another with herbs.
After four years of study, individuals become
members by examination. Current membership:
150)

School of Health
Mountain Grove
Glendale, Ore. 97442
(Teaches health not healing; includes an herb mainte-
nance program)

Stellar Energy Exchange
P.O. Box 802
Monte Rio, Calif. 95462
(Offers classes in herbology)

Tara (Temple of the Divine Mother)
P.O. Box 604
Ukiah, Calif. 95482
(Offers workshops in herbology training; available to
spiritual groups and individuals)

Wholistic Healing Center
c/o All One Family Union
P.O. Box 7705
San Diego, Calif. 92107
(Join a farming community as a resident herbalist!
This is a temporary address; add "please forward"
to the envelope.)

Yarrow
P.O. Box 16153
Sacramento, Calif. 95816
(Study with an herbalist with five years of indepen-
    dent study; eclectic healing techniques)

For information on medical practices using herbs
write

The Naturopath
1920 N. Kilpatrick Street
Portland, Ore. 97208
(Will provide a list of teachers and schools)

Homeopathic Information Service
c/o The American Institute of Homeopathy
P.O. Box 44
Chestnut Hill, Mass. 02167

WHN (Wholistic Health and Nutrition Institute)
150 Shoreline Hwy.
Mill Valley, Calif. 94941
(A non-profit educational organization with which you
    may link up as teacher or student)

Caraway

Afterword

All herbs ask is attention. And there's a bountiful reward to be reaped. Health. Wealth. And a link in the chain of history. The interest in herbs is growing. Perhaps they will be a staple of the good life to come, as taken for granted in the future as they have been neglected in the past.

Let's hope, in service of evolution, that we place herbs out front. This book is my part. And, now, to you . . .

Sources and resources

This is information for you and acknowledgment of those whose help brought this book into being. The following organizations and companies graciously responded to my inquiries:

Attar Herbs and Spices
Smith Village
New Ipswich, N.H. 03071

Comstock, Ferre & Co.
263 Main St.
Wethersfield, Conn. 06109
(buy on contract from growers in U.S. and Europe)

Dharma Trading Co.
Box 06447
Portland, Ore. 97206
(wholesale and mail order ginseng)

Eden Foods
4601 Platt Road
Ann Arbor, Mich. 48104

Green Valley Seeds
11565 N.E. Zayante
Felton, Calif. 95018
(organic seeds for sprouting, herbs & ginseng; "service
   without profit"—send a stamp for catalog)

Herbarium, Inc.
Route 2, Box 620
Kenosha, Wis. 53104
(importers/exporters of botanical drugs and spices)

Indiana Botanic Gardens, Inc.
P.O. Box 5
Hammond, Ind. 46325
(botanical and herbal products; catalog 25¢)

Infinity Herbal Products, Ltd.
42 Eugene Street
Toronto, Ont.
M6B 3Z4
Canada
(uses herbs in preparing hair care products and soaps)

Joyful Herb Shop
5713 W. Belmont Ave.
Chicago, Ill. 60634

Le Jardin du Gourmet
West Danville, Vt. 05873
(seeds from France)

Nichols Garden Nursery
1190 N. Pacific Highway
Albany, Ore. 97321
(strong in educating others to be herb growers; dealers
in seeds, plants and herb products, etc.)

Pure Planet
Box 675
North Tempe, Ariz. 85281
(goldenseal, ginseng, pollens, etc.)

Sunshine Natural Products
Box NA
Renick, W.Va. 24966
(natural cosmetics)

The following may also boost your growing herb and
herb-growing interest:

Dr. Michael's Herb Center
1223 N. Milwaukee Avenue
Chicago, Ill. 60622
(full line of medicinal herbs)

The Fir Tree
P.O. Box 130
Mi-Wuk, Calif. 95346
(seeds, cones, pods, beans, grasses, acorns)

Floral Art
Main Street
Dennis, Mass. 02638
(dried herbs and accessories)

The Golden Unicorn
22 Rustic Drive
Howell Township
Lakewood, N. J. 08701
(supplier of dry weeds, seeds, pods; catalog 50¢)

Herbal Aphrodisiacs
Dept. 96D
320 Ocean
Oxnard, Calif. 93030

Herbal Pathways
Box 815, Dept. B
Wayne, N.J. 07470
(herbal smoking products)

Herbs and Spiritual Healing Center
Garden of Sanjivani
2083 Ocean Street
Santa Cruz, Calif. 95060
(herb work-study apprentice program; 1977 tuition,
    $350 per month, residential, $150, nonresidential)

Herbs Etc.
652 Canyon Road
Santa Fe, N.M. 87501
(13-day "Learning Vacation" in practical use of herbs;
    1977 "tuition," $85)

Lamb's End
16861 Hamilton
Highland Park, Mich. 48203
(dyes, mordants, fibers, yarn, books)

Meadowbrook Herb Garden
Wyoming, R.I. 02898
(an organic herb garden; catalog 50¢)

Natural Dye Supplies
P.O. Box 7
Pelham, N.Y. 10803
(mordants)

True Seed Exchange
c/o Kent Whealy
R.F.D. 2 (MA)
Princeton, Mo. 64673
(source for seed bartering; newsletter including infor-
    mation on saving seeds and exchanging with oth-
    ers is $1. Club membership is 140)

Shepard and Linnette Erhart
Franklin, Maine 04634
(source and potential market for seaweeds)

Finally, there are the freebies. The following is a list
of publications for nothing or next to it. They cover
everything from the psychology of advertising to how
to build a garden shed.

"The New Psychology of Advertising and Selling"
The Hopkins Syndicate Inc.
Hopkins Building
Mellott, Ind. 47958
(booklet on how to advertise and sell your goods; 25¢)

"Where & How to Get a Farm"
(#L432)
Publications
Office of Communication
U.S. Dept. of Agriculture
Washington, D.C. 20250

"Emergency Loans"
(#PA490)U.S. Dept. of Agriculture
(see above address)
(A companion piece to the above; informs new and old
      farmers on what money is available and how to
      get it.)

Merchandisers Digest Magazine
Box 37313
Cincinnati, Ohio 45237
(a quarterly dedicated to mail order, retail, wholesale,
      door-to-door, party plans and other means to make
      money; send a self-addressed, stamped envelope
      for a sample copy)

"Need a Little Help?" (#PA706)
U.S. Dept. of Agriculture
(see above address)
(advice on making more money farming and starting a
      small business)

"Cooperatives: What are They?"
American Institute of Cooperation
1129 20th Street, NW
Washington, D.C. 20036
(tells how co-ops work)

Georgia-Pacific Corporation
900 S.W. Fifth Avenue
Portland, Ore. 97204
or
Z-Brick Company
Division V.M.C. Corp.
Woodinville, Wash. 98072
   (instructions on how to build your own garden or
storage shed. Georgia-Pacific pamphlet is 25¢; Z-
Brick's is 10¢)

Bibliography

The following publications were invaluable in my search for the "truth" about herbs. Most of the books, listed first, include sources from which you may seek even more information about herbs.

Books

Andrews, Edward Deming and Faith. *Fruits of the Shaker Life Tree.* Stockbridge, Mass.: Berkshire Traveler Press, 1975.

Bernath, Stefen. *Herbs Coloring Book.* New York: Dover Publishing, Inc., 1976.

Brooklyn Botanic Garden. *Dried Flower Designs: Plants and Gardens,* Vol. 30, No. 3. Brooklyn, 1974.

Brownlow, Margaret. The *Delights of Herb Growing. Gestetner Duplications* (B.S.O.), Ltd. 19.
(B.S.O.), Ltd. 19

Common Weeds of the United States. Washington: U.S. Department of Agriculture.

Conway, David. *The Magic of Herbs.* London: Jonathon Cape, 1973.

Findhorn Community, The. 2The Findhorn Garden.1 New York: Harper Row, 1975.

Gibbons, Euell. *Stalking the Blue-Eyed Scallop.* New York: David McKay Co., 1964.

Stalking the Healthful Herbs. New York: David McKay Co., 1966.

Grieve, Mrs. M. *A Modern Herbal,* Vols. 1 and 2. New York: Dover Publications, 1971.

Harris, Ben C. *Eat the Weeds.* New Cannan, Conn.: Keas Publishing, Inc., 1972.

Hatfield, Audrey Wynne. *How to Enjoy Your Weeds.* New York: Collier Books, 1971.

Huson, Paul. *Mastering Herbalism.* New York: Stein and Day, 1974.

Hylton, William H., editor. *The Rodale Herb Book.* Emmaus, Pa.: Rodale Press Book Division, 1974.

Jacobs, Betty E.M. *Profitable Herb Growing at Home.* Charlotte, Vt.: Garden Way Publishing, 1976.

Kadans, Joseph M. *Modern Encyclopedia of Herbs.* West Nyack, N.Y.: Parker Publishing Co., 1970.

Kierstead, Sallie Place. *Natural Dyes.* Boston: Branden Press, Inc., 1950.

Kloss, Jethro. *Back to Eden.* Santa Barbara, Calif.: Woodbridge Press Publishing Co., 1972.

Leyel, C.F. *Elixirs of Life.* New York: Samuel Weiser, Inc. 1970.

Macmanima, George. *Dry It—You'll Like It.* Fall City, Wash., Living Foods Dehydrators, 1973.

Nichols, N.P. *Profitable Herb Growing.* Albany, Ore.: Nichols Garden Nursery, 97321.

O'Brien, Marian M. *The Bible Herb Book,* St. Louis, Bethany Press, 1960.

Pathways to Wholeness: A Healing Guide. Berkeley,

Calif.: Clear Life Publishers, 1976. (A guide to West Coast healers and herbalists.)

Plummer, Beverly. *Earth Presents: How to Make Beautiful Gifts from Nature's Bounty*. New York: A. & W. Visual Library, 1974.

Rose, Jeanne. *Herbs & Things: Jeanne Rose's Herbal*. New York: Workman Publishing Co., Grosset & Dunlap, 1972

Simmons, Adelma Grenier. *Herb Gardening in Five Seasons*. Princeton, N.J.: Van Nostrand Co., Inc., 1964.

Simmons, Adelma Grenier, *Herbs to Grow Indoors*. New York: Hawthorn Books, 1969.

Stevenson, Violet. *A Modern Herbal*. London: Lynx Press Ltd., 1974.

Tobe, John H. *Proven Herbal Remedies*. Provoker Press, 1969.

Vogel, Virgil J. *American Indian Medicine*. Norman, Okla.: University of Oklahoma Press, 1970.

Wickham, Cynthia. *Herbs*. London: Marshall Cavendish Publishers, Ltd., 1975.

Wigginton, Elliot. *Foxfire 3*. Garden City, N.Y.: Anchor Press/Doubleday, 1975.

Wilson, Charles Marrow. *Roots: Miracles Below*. Garden City, N.Y.: Doubleday, o8

Periodicals

The world of herbs changes almost daily. Plants come in and out of popularity due to fickle fate and special interests by herbal practitioners. You might check the following publications now and again to see what they report on herbs, their cultivation, popularity, profit, and use. You'll learn a lot about related subjects, too.

The Mother Earth News, P.O. Box 70, Hendersonville, N.C., 28739. (Subscription rate: $10 per year, 6 issues).

Organic Gardening and Farming, Rodale Press, Inc., 33 E. Minor St., Emmaus, Pa. 18049. ($7.85 per year, monthly).

Harrowsmith, Camden House Publishing, Camden East, Ontario K0K 1J0, Canada. ($6 per year, 6 issues).

Farmstead Magazine: Home Gardening & Small Farming, The Farmstead Press, P.O. Box 111, Freedom, Maine 04941. ($6 per year, 6 issues).

The *CoEvolution Quarterly,* Point, Box 428, Sausalito, Calif. 94965. ($8 per year, quarterly).

Prevention: A Magazine for Better Health, Rodale Press, Inc., 33 E. Minor Street, Emmaus, Pa. 18049. ($7.85 per year, monthly).

New Age Magazine, Subscriptions Dept. P.O. Box 4921, Manchester, N.H. 03108. ($12 a year, monthly).

Come Out, Outdoor Living International, Box 1283, Madison, Tenn. 37115. ($5 per year, 6 issues).

The *Herbalist Almanac,* The Indiana Botanical Gardens, P.O. Box 5, Hammond, Ind. 46325. (Subscription: free with order, annual).

The *Herbalist,* BiWorld Publishers, Inc., 224 N. Draper Lane, P.O. Box 62, Provo, Utah 84601. ($9 per year, monthly).

Well-Being Magazine, Well-Being Productions, 833 W. Fir Street, San Diego, Calif. 92101. ($10, annual).

Index